# GREAT RACES

# GREAT RACES

SEAN MAGEE

Anaya Publishers Ltd
London

First published in Great Britain 1990
by Anaya Publishers Ltd, 49 Neal Street, London WC2H 9PJ

**British Library Cataloguing in Publication Data**
Magee, Sean
    Great races.
    1. Racehorses. Racing. Races. History
    I. Title
    798.4009
ISBN 1 85470 016 2 (hb)
        1 85470 066 9 (pb)

Managing Editor: Barbara Horn
Editor: Gillian Bromley
Designer: Bob Hook
Picture Researcher: Andrea Stern

Typeset by Tradespools Ltd, Frome, Somerset
Colour reproduction by Columbia Offset, Singapore
Printed and bound in Great Britain by Clays Ltd., Bungay, Suffolk

FRONTISPIECE *Nashwan (left) and Cacoethes go clear in the King George VI
and Queen Elizabeth Diamond Stakes, Ascot, July 1989.*

# CONTENTS

*You* know *when a contest between horses has booked itself a permanent place in the annals. And if you have witnessed it in the flesh you simply want to be able to say, to anyone who may wish to listen: "I was there."*

# INTRODUCTION

Saturday 26 July 1975 was hot and sunny, no day to be caught in a traffic jam. Yet for thousands of racegoers inching their way towards Ascot and finding that hours before the first race the cars were already backed up miles from the track, the hold-up was no more than a minor irritation. We appreciated the reason for the crush: the Derby winner Grundy was being pitched in against the likes of Dahlia, Bustino, Star Appeal and Ashmore in the King George VI and Queen Elizabeth Diamond Stakes. We were going to see a great race.

It was not until some hours later that we knew just how great a race, but no one could have driven away from Ascot later that day without knowing that they had witnessed something quite unforgettable, a contest which would live on in the recollections of racing fans for as long as the sport is talked about and written about.

Fourteen years later the season and the weather were very different, but the anticipation was the same, and as we splashed through the snow-covered Cotswolds towards Cheltenham one topic dominated the conversation: could Desert Orchid overcome the dreadful conditions and his dislike of the track to win the Gold Cup and proclaim himself one of the all-time great steeplechasers? He could.

One year on, in March 1990, the weather was much more clement for that drive to Cheltenham on the Thursday of the Festival meeting – warm, sunny and springlike. By then forty-nine of the fifty races demanded for this book had been selected, but though the deadline for delivery of the text was fast approaching I had left one slot free in case the 1990 Festival Meeting should throw up a last-minute candidate. The first two days had produced marvellous sport and some stirring finishes but nothing which quite qualified. The final day would hardly help, for was not the Gold Cup no more than a benefit for the doted-upon Desert Orchid? If he had won the race last year in such foul conditions, how could he possibly lose with the sun on his back today? It seemed as if it would be necessary after all to delve back into history for that fiftieth race, but as I travelled towards Cheltenham that morning, rescue was at hand in the shape of a horse who had already arrived at the course, driven from his stable (a converted milking shed) on a Welsh dairy farm, with his owner-trainer at the wheel of the horsebox. That horse would provide the needed great race.

Those three occasions characterize the three sections into which the races chronicled in the following pages have been divided. The sections are not mutually exclusive, but seemed a convenient way to express what made the events within them worthy of remembering.

'Head to Head' is concerned with eighteen races which live on in racing memory primarily on account of the stirring finishes they produced. Many of the finishes were desperately close – Affirmed and Alydar, Northern Dancer and Hill Rise, Special Cargo, Lettoch and Diamond Edge – but not all: Arkle won the 1964 Gold Cup by five lengths, Brigadier Gerard the 1971 Two Thousand Guineas by three, yet such races find a place in this section as they were showdowns between great horses.

'Star Turns' offers accounts of twenty races which produced performances of outstanding individual brilliance, races which confirmed the standing of the winner as one of the all-time greats or (as in the case of Teleprompter's victory in the 1985 Arlington Million) ensured a niche for that horse in racing history. And in one case – still painful to recall – the race prepared a niche for two horses, one for the gallant but defeated Crisp, the other for his conqueror Red Rum: the triple Grand National winner doubtless deserves an entry all to himself, but it is intended as no slight on his achievements that here he is bracketed with his most notable Liverpool victim for his part in a contest which in greatness outshone his two subsequent National triumphs.

The third section – 'A Sense of Occasion' – describes twelve races. It may be straining the notion of what is 'great' to include such events as Foinavon's Grand National ('an awful race' for trainer Peter Cazalet) or the controversial 1968 Washington International alongside the joyous moments like Gordon Richards's Derby triumph in 1953 or Bob Champion's 1981 Grand National, but those races are remembered as big occasions which somehow went sour, and must have their place.

To a degree all such categories are arbitrary, but however we may group these milestones along the ever-unfolding history of the Turf around the world the question remains: what makes a race great? The notion of greatness itself is of course a dubious one, for each person brings to each race his or her own notion of eligibility, but the concept reduces to a simple gut feeling: you *know* when a contest between horses has booked itself a permanent place in the annals. And if you have witnessed it in the flesh you simply want to be able to say, to anyone who may wish to listen: 'I was there.'

I was there for many of the races described in this book. When I have not been there (usually on account of geography or history), I have – where possible – watched on television or studied film of the race. I make no apology for including two victories by Arkle – the only horse to be so honoured – for he was a horse quite apart, but my recollection of the moment when he strolled past Mill House in the 1965 Gallaher Gold Cup cannot be supported by re-watching a film of the race, as despite strenuous efforts I have not been able to find surviving footage. I saw him in the flesh only once, at Kempton Park in December 1965, but that was enough to confirm my teenage opinion that he was a god among horses.

I have met many of the other horses featured in this book in their later years – Nijinsky, Red Rum, Sir Ivor, Royal Palace, Secretariat – as well as some of those (such as Blakeney) who played supporting roles, and always the memory rewinds to the moments when they reserved their place in racing history. On the whole, it is great horses who make great races – and sometimes it is great races that make great horses. But there is also the human element, and the moments of glory of Gordon Richards and Lester Piggott have a rightful claim to be included.

We like – we need – to know about the great races of the past, as they form the benchmarks by which we will judge the races of the future. Hugh McIlvanney, writing about Secretariat's all but unbelievable win in the 1978 Belmont Stakes, caught exactly their appeal:

'None of us can ever expect to see the like of that again. But let's go on climbing up into the stands, just in case.'

*Grundy and Bustino fight out the finish of the 1975 King George VI and Queen Elizabeth Diamond Stakes at Ascot.*

# HEAD TO HEAD

# GRUNDY AND BUSTINO

*❛ He fought me back like a lion ❜*

Ascot racecourse on a burning July afternoon. The runners are about to leave the paddock for the King George VI and Queen Elizabeth Diamond Stakes, the most important race of the British Flat season. Since its inception in 1951, the King George has rarely failed to fulfil its aim of bringing the very best of Europe's middle-distance horses – at three years and over – into contention, and as the field sorts itself into racecard order for the parade which will precede the race, the atmosphere is heavy with excitement and expectation. For while the King George always produces a memorable race, today's field is of such quality, and the possibilities which the race holds so varied, that the air crackles with that tension unique to an occasion when something very special is about to happen.

The horse leading the runners past the packed stands is Ashmore, a high-class French four-year-old. Owned by Daniel Wildenstein, trained by Angel Penna and ridden by Yves Saint-Martin, he won the Prix Jean de Chaudenay at Saint-Cloud in May and then ran a gallant second in the Coronation Cup at Epsom, fighting for three furlongs to get his head in front before going down by a length to Bustino, the previous year's St Leger winner. And it is Bustino who follows Ashmore in the parade, a tall, strong, superbly well built bay four-year-old bred by his owner Lady Beaverbrook, trained by Dick Hern and ridden by Joe Mercer. Bustino's forte is stamina – as his St Leger victory showed – but he's pretty speedy too: his victory in the Coronation Cup, his only previous race this season, set a course record. It is vital to his chance in the King George that a strong pace is made to draw the sting of some of his rivals with more instant acceleration, and behind him in the parade are two horses who are there to ensure that those rivals hardly get the chance to draw breath.

But immediately behind Bustino is Card King, another French challenger. He is a seven-year-old who has already run three times in the Prix de l'Arc de Triomphe – fourth to Rheingold in 1973 his best placing – and who earlier this season won the important Prix d'Harcourt at Longchamp and ran second to Allez France in the Prix Ganay at the same course. Behind him comes Kin-glet, a decent middle-distance handicapper but completely outclassed in this company. That, however, is not the point, for four-year-old Kinglet is one of Bustino's pacemakers. Bustino's usual pacemaker is the good four-year-old Riboson, who did the job in the 1974 St Leger and was stout enough in his own right to keep on and finish third. He had also set the pace in Bustino's record-breaking Coronation Cup, but since then has broken a cannon bone and is out of action. In his stead Bustino's connections have worked out a strategy which involves two other horses, and Kinglet will be required to keep up a furious gallop as soon as the first pacemaker is burnt out and to see that there is no breather before Bustino takes up the running at or about the final bend, less than three furlongs out. Kinglet is ridden by Eric Eldin, who like Joe Mercer wears Lady Beaverbrook's colours of 'beaver brown, maple leaf green cross-belts'; but Mercer sports the first colours and wears a maple leaf green cap: Eldin's is a distinguishing red.

Then comes the five-year-old On My Way, trained in France and ridden by the Australian jockey Bill Pyers. Although unplaced in the 1974 Arc behind Allez France, On My Way has some top-rate form, notably victory in the Prix du Prince d'Orange last autumn; but he has not won yet in four races this season. Behind him is another five-year-old, Star Appeal; trained in Germany by Theo Greiper and ridden by Greville Starkey, he epitomizes the international nature of modern racing, for the three races he has won this season before coming to Ascot are the Grosser Preis der Badischen Wirtschaft at Baden-Baden, the Gran Premio di Milano at San Siro, and the Benson and Hedges Eclipse Stakes at Sandown Park earlier in the month, when he started at 20–1 and beat Nobiliary, second to Grundy in the Derby.

In contrast to the '111' form figures by Star Appeal's name in the racecard, the big, rangy mare who follows him in the parade sports seasonal figures of '0000'. But this is Dahlia, one of the toughest and most popular mares seen in Europe since the war. Now five, she sprang upon the international scene when a dazzling burst of acceleration brought her the Irish Guinness Oaks in 1973, and one week later repeated the performance to win

*The jockeys leave the weighing room: Joe Mercer (Bustino) is second from the left and Pat Eddery (Grundy) on the extreme right.*

the King George itself. In 1974 she became the only horse to win the great Ascot race twice and then took the Benson and Hedges Gold Cup at York; by the end of the 1974 season she had won major races in France, England, Ireland, the USA (including the Washington International) and Canada and prize money of £458,344, setting a record for a European-trained horse. If this season so far has been a disappointment, her run last time out when fifth in the Grand Prix de Saint-Cloud after being hampered on the final bend suggested that she might just be coming back to form, and Lester Piggott has the mount. But she has been showing signs of temperament in recent races and now, as the parade goes on, she is continuing to sweat up. Then there's the four-year-old filly Dibidale, a spectacularly unlucky loser of last year's Oaks when her saddle slipped round her belly in the closing stages: after that misfortune she showed just how good she can be by winning the Irish Guinness Oaks and the Yorkshire Oaks. Three runs this season have brought a third in the

Jockey Club Stakes at Newmarket and the same position in the Hardwicke Stakes at Royal Ascot; on her most recent outing she ran last in the Grand Prix de Saint-Cloud, with four of today's runners – Ashmore, On My Way, Dahlia and Card King – in front.

Next: Grundy. A bright chestnut with a distinctive crooked white blaze down his nose, he is the smallest horse in the field but looks outstanding: muscular and perfectly balanced, keyed up and sweating slightly, he is the picture of health and has been trained to perfection by Peter Walwyn for Italian owner Carlo Vittadini (whose daughter Franca earlier this afternoon rode the winner of the ladies' race). Irish-born Pat Eddery, who was champion jockey for the first time last season, is in the saddle. He has ridden Grundy in all his outings, and this will be their tenth contest together. Unbeaten in four races as a two-year-old including the Champagne Stakes at Doncaster and the Dewhurst Stakes at Newmarket, Grundy has developed into a three-year-old of the highest class. Although second to Bolkonski in

*Grundy holds on as Bustino fights back.*

*An exhausted Grundy returns to the unsaddling enclosure.*

the Two Thousand Guineas after a training setback (he was kicked in the face by another horse during preparation for his pre-Guineas race at Newbury), he won the Irish Two Thousand and then put up a superb performance in the Derby, coming home three lengths clear of the filly Nobiliary. After that came a trip to The Curragh for an easy victory in the Irish Sweeps Derby from King Pellinore. Grundy seems to be an above-average Derby winner; his King George performance will show just how good he is.

Behind Grundy are two more three-year-olds, like him receiving a stone in weight from their elders. Highest is the other pacemaker for Bustino: he has to set a scorching pace for as long as he can before giving way to Kinglet, and his jockey Frankie Durr is also wearing Lady Beaverbrook's colours, this time with a black cap. And bringing up the rear is Libra's Rib, who seems to be improving: he was second in the King Edward VII Stakes at Royal Ascot and on his last outing won the Princess of Wales's Stakes at Newmarket's July Meeting.

Eleven runners. Though their respective chances of lifting the £81,910 first prize are still being feverishly discussed as the runners reach the end of the parade and turn to canter back to the one-and-a-half-mile start, most spectators are keener on finding and holding a good viewing position than rushing down to the betting ring for a last-minute investment. Bustino's appearance is magnificent, and he strides majestically down to the start. But Grundy looks no less well and his form is of a high order: as the Derby winner canters keenly past the stands, head held high, his price in the ring hardens from 11–10 against to odds-on. Bustino is second favourite, Dahlia third choice — more on the strength of her record than her current form — and Star Appeal and Ashmore are attracting a little interest. You can name your own price about the pacemakers.

At the start, some of the runners seek shelter from the glare of the sun under the trees which line the far side of the course all the way down to the long, sweeping bend at Swinley Bottom. On My Way has cantered on nearly as far as the one-and-a-quarter-mile start, and as he strolls back to rejoin his rivals a quiet descends on the stands. Bustino is behaving with wonted placidness and Grundy, though still sweating slightly and anxious to get on with it, is calm enough — unlike Dahlia, who is not on good terms with herself. Piggott has to dismount while she plays up, but she is treated with infinite patience by the stalls handlers and eventually consents to go in. All the others are loaded quickly and without fuss. Grundy is 5–4 on favourite, with Bustino at 4–1, Dahlia 6–1, Star Appeal 13–1 and Ashmore 18–1. The rear gate is slammed shut behind the last horse. The white flag is up: under starter's orders. Starter Michael Eveleigh presses his lever and the gates snap open. They're off.

The first move is quite unexpected – Bustino shoots out of his stall and for a few strides has the lead. This is not at all what is wanted, but soon the carefully laid plan is working out, for Durr has pushed Highest to the front. For three furlongs the field rushes down towards Swinley Bottom at an astonishing rate for a mile-and-a-half race, and several of the runners are already at full stretch – not least the leader Highest, being pushed along on the rails by Durr clear from his two stable-companions, Kinglet second and Bustino third. As they start to swing right-handed Greville Starkey brings Star Appeal up into third, and halfway round the turn Highest has had enough, dropping back to let Kinglet take over. But the breakneck pace does not slacken as the runners straighten up and climb out of Swinley Bottom towards the turn into the home straight. Eldin on Kinglet is pushing for all he is worth, Bustino is poised behind him, Star Appeal is still there in third, Dahlia is running sweetly in fourth and Grundy is well in touch. But Kinglet, out of his depth in terms of ability and exhausted from having had to run a mile faster than he's ever been called upon to do, cannot stay in front of the best horses in Europe for long, and as they near the straight he is coming to to the end of his tether. Joe Mercer on Bustino is alive to the position, and with half a mile to go the St Leger winner accelerates smoothly into the lead. It may be sooner than Mercer Ideally would like but Bustino is going so well that there is no point in delaying. From here on the strategy is simple: catch me if you can!

Ascot
1½ miles
26 July 1975

| 1 Grundy | P. Eddery | 4–5 fav. |
| 2 Bustino | J. Mercer | 4–1 |
| 3 Dahlia | L. Piggott | 6–1 |

*Also ran:* On My Way (4th), Card King, Star
Appeal, Ashmore, Dibidale, Libra's Rib,
Kinglet, Highest

11 ran

Winner owned by C. Vittadini, trained by P.
Walwyn

*Distances:* ½ length, 5 lengths

*Grundy starts to get his breath
back.*

Pat Eddery on Grundy is also well aware of
how the race is unfolding, and as Bustino
accelerates he asks his mount to go after
him. So fast is the leader galloping that
Grundy cannot instantly match Bustino's
burst of speed, and Eddery has to ride hard
to pass Star Appeal, who then gives up third
place to Dahlia as Piggott tries to get the
mare on terms. As the bell clangs to
announce that the runners are swinging into
the straight Bustino has the rails and is four
lengths up; Grundy is chasing him hard but
making no obvious impression, Dahlia is a
clear third and the rest are beaten off. In the
home straight, with just two and a half furlongs to go, Bustino, the confirmed stayer, is
showing no signs of stopping, and as Mercer,
disdaining the use of the whip on a partner
who is already giving his best, drives him for
home it looks as if Grundy is in trouble, for
Eddery gets to work with his stick. But the
gap is gradually being whittled away, and
there are now only two furlongs to go. Can
Grundy get there? Again Grundy feels the
sting of the whip, and digs deep to find more
strength and more courage. Find them he
does, and draws closer and closer, so that
with a furlong to go he is all but level with his
rival and has generated the momentum
which should take him on to a hard-fought
but clear-cut victory. Just inside the final furlong Grundy is upsides, but Bustino refuses
to capitulate and Grundy's appearing in his
line of vision seems to spur him to yet greater effort. As Grundy takes a slight lead Bustino, tongue lolling out in his final effort,
rallies and nearly claws back the deficit. For a
hundred yards they are neck and neck, both
flat out. Then Bustino, dead tired, starts to
falter. He rolls away from the rails towards
Grundy, but heroically as he battles to get
back he just cannot do so, and with fifty
yards to go his energy has drained away and
he has to admit defeat. At the winning post
Grundy is half a length up.

The final stages of the race have been
enveloped in a euphoria of cheering –
though plenty of those present have been so
moved by the spectacle that they have
simply watched in dumbstruck awe – and as
the noise subsides into a babble of elated
appreciation and analysis the runners pull
up. Grundy, three minutes earlier the picture of health and readiness, is now the picture of exhaustion – covered in sweat and
drained of all energy, he stands stock still,
head down, for a moment before turning to
come back. People stampede from the
stands, rush down the stairs, shove their way
down the escalators; from Tattersalls they
race along the tunnel to get to the unsaddling enclosure, for they must be there.
When Grundy and Bustino are led in, with
Dahlia (third) and On My Way (fourth), the
cheers ring out long and loud. These spectators cramming and pushing to greet the two
heroes know that they have seen as great a
race as they are ever likely to witness. The
time of the race, when it comes, is no surprise: 2 minutes 26.98 seconds beats the
previous course record for a mile and a half
by 2.36 seconds and is the fastest twelve furlongs ever electrically recorded in Britain.
That record will be broken before very long,
but the fame of this race will last, and already
many seasoned racegoers are describing it as
the greatest race they ever saw ...

That view was confirmed by the journalists.
For Brough Scott in the *Sunday Times* it was
'the hardest, most implacable, most moving
flat race that I have ever seen'. For Hugh
McIlvanney in *The Observer*, 'a glittering,
flawless example of horse racing at its most
irresistible'. Christopher Hawkins wrote a
whole book about the race, its title reflecting
the terms in which the 1975 King George
and Queen Elizabeth Diamond Stakes will go
down in history: *The Race of the Century*.

More immediately came opinions from
those most directly involved. Winning
jockey Pat Eddery described his feelings as
Bustino went clear on the approach to the
home turn: 'When Joe asked Bustino to
quicken, I just couldn't go with him as he
took the lead. Bustino must have had four
lengths on me going to the turn. I got my fellow going once we were in the straight and
reached Bustino about a furlong from home.
But he fought me back like a lion – and hon-
estly I didn't know which of us would win.
Then, about fifty yards from home, Bustino
cracked. What great horses they both are.'
Joe Mercer reported how 'four furlongs out I
was going so easy that I thought, "Right, I'm
off." Turning into the straight I knew it

would take a hell of a horse to beat me but in the final hundred yards Bustino faltered.' Years later Mercer elaborated on why he thinks his mount lost his stride: 'Bustino got beaten because he broke down half a furlong from home. He only cantered once after that. His tendon had gone and that was it. If you watch the race, he's winning, winning, winning. Then all of a sudden he changes his legs, his tongue comes out and he rolls to one side. At the time, yes, I thought we'd been beaten by the better horse, but make no mistake, Grundy was a hell of a race-horse.' Bustino's trainer Dick Hern declared himself 'as proud of Bustino as if he'd won. I think he might just have done it if Riboson had been there to lead him into the straight. Bustino was in front a long time and it proved just too much for him in the end.' Bustino's owner Lady Beaverbrook also lamented the absence of Riboson but confessed how her horse 'filled me with pride as well as heartache'.

Bustino did not run again, an injury during his preparation for the Prix de l'Arc de Triomphe hastening his retirement to stud. Grundy, thought to have recovered well from the rigours of this race, took on some of the horses he had beaten at Ascot in the Benson and Hedges Gold Cup at York just over three weeks later. But he ran a lifeless race and finished fourth behind Dahlia, Card King and Star Appeal, all well beaten in the King George. That was his final racecourse appearance.

Significantly, the weight-for-age scale was amended in 1976 to stipulate that a four-year-old facing a three-year-old over one and a half miles in late July concedes one pound less than the stone which Bustino gave to Grundy; form experts speculated about what would have happened in the King George if the difference had only been thirteen pounds on 26 July 1975.

... But all that lies ahead. Now, on a shimmering afternoon, the afterglow infuses all at Ascot as Grundy and Bustino – whose names will henceforth be bracketed whenever the talk is of famous races – are brought in. Joe Mercer pulls the saddle off Bustino and makes for the steps down to the weighing room. As he passes the horse's head he pulls affectionately at Bustino's left ear. Well run.

# AFFIRMED AND ALYDAR

*Belmont Stakes*
*Belmont Park, 10 June 1978*

Affirmed and Alydar raced against each other on ten occasions. The ninth of these, the 1978 Belmont Stakes, produced one of the most monumental struggles ever seen in American racing.

Affirmed, trained by Laz Barrera, was a narrow-framed, lanky chestnut with an iron constitution who showed the courage of a lion on the track. Off it he was calm and untroubled, and was in the habit of taking an afternoon nap in his stall, during which he would wiggle his ears, a habit he also showed in races. He was not long into his racing career before dreams of his great rival Alydar would set his ears a-wiggling.

Alydar himself was quite a character, if his relationship with his regular jockey Jorge Velasquez was anything to go by. 'The relationship between Alydar and me was unbelievable,' Velasquez would recall: 'I used to hide behind a tree and call him. I made him crazy, bucking and kicking inside his stall looking for me.'

The two colts first met as two-year-olds early in 1977. In the Youthful Stakes three other horses divided Affirmed's first place from Alydar's fifth. It was Alydar's debut, and he learned enough from the experience to run up a sequence of four victories before meeting Affirmed again in the Great American Stakes. This time Alydar won. Affirmed then won the Hollywood Juvenile by seven lengths and the Sanford Stakes at Saratoga before engaging in the four races with Alydar which established their intense rivalry. In the Hopeful Stakes, Alydar was favourite but Affirmed won by half a length. In the Futurity Stakes at Belmont Park the seventeen-year-old Steve Cauthen conjured a winning run out of Affirmed after he had been headed by Alydar in the home stretch: Affirmed won by a nose, with the third horse eleven lengths in arrears. Then to the Champagne Stakes, where Jorge Velasquez replaced Eddie Maple on Alydar, and the switch paid off. Alydar beat Affirmed by one and a quarter lengths, though Cauthen ascribed Affirmed's defeat to the horse's being too concerned with beating another runner: 'He had plenty left, but he was so busy playing games with Darby Creek Road that he never even saw Alydar until it was too late.' Their final encounter as two-year-olds came in the Laurel Futurity in Maryland in late October, when after a ferocious battle Affirmed just got his head in front.

Six clashes, and the score was four–two to Affirmed. He it was who took the Eclipse Award as top two-year-old colt, but many felt that Alydar would turn out to be better at three: he had the more classic physique of the two, and would probably prove superior at the longer distances of the Triple Crown races. To open his three-year-old season Alydar's trainer John Veitch sent him out to win three races in Florida, including the Florida Derby, and then on to Keeneland, where he won the Blue Grass Stakes by thirteen lengths. Meanwhile Affirmed had been in California and won four races, the Santa Anita Derby and the Hollywood Derby among them.

The rivals met again at Churchill Downs in the Kentucky Derby. Alydar was favourite but it was Affirmed who got first run as his rival hung at the back of the field, and by the time Alydar got going it was too late, Affirmed winning by one and a half lengths. In the Preakness two weeks later Steve Cauthen sent Affirmed into the lead early. At the top of the home stretch Velasquez brought Alydar to challenge; though he cut back the deficit, again he could not get past Affirmed, who was a neck up at the wire.

So when they lined up in the Belmont Stakes for their ninth meeting, Cauthen on Affirmed, Velasquez on Alydar, the score read: Affirmed six, Alydar two. Now Affirmed was going for his Triple Crown, but Alydar had reduced the length-and-a-half deficit in the Kentucky Derby to a neck in the Preakness, and the result was no foregone conclusion.

By the time the field had swung round the first turn and were straightening out for the long back stretch the two principals were already locked together, and for the final mile of the most gruelling and demanding leg of the Triple Crown they were inseparable. They thundered along the back stretch flat out, neck and neck, nose and nose. Affirmed had the advantage of the inside, and as they charged off the final turn he wiggled his ears as Alydar came nearer. Straightened up and going for home, Alydar started to launch his finishing run on the stands side as

**◀ It was a real horse race, all right ▶**

*Head to head, Affirmed (right)
and Alydar go for the finish.*

**Belmont Stakes**

Belmont Park
1¹/₂ miles
10 June 1978

| | | |
|---|---|---|
| 1 Affirmed | S. Cauthen | 6–10 fav. |
| 2 Alydar | J. Velasquez | 11–10 |
| 3 Darby Creek Road | A. Cordero | 99–10 |

*Also ran:* Judge Advocate (4th), Noon Time
Spender

5 ran

Winner owned by Harbor View Farm,
trained by L. Barrera

*Distances:* head, 13³/₄ lengths

Affirmed plugged gamely on, the two well clear of the other runners. Affirmed had had a hard season; might he have lost his edge? As Cauthen stole a glance to his right and saw Alydar's stretched-out head edging into sight he cannot have been very confident that his horse would have more to find. Then his worst fears were realized as Affirmed started to tire at the three-sixteenths pole and Alydar got his nose in front. Cauthen's whip was in his left hand, Velasquez had his in his right, and with their sticks flailing the two plumbed the depths of their horses' resolution. Affirmed was more tired than he had ever been but still responded to Cauthen's driving finish, and started to claw his way back. With less than fifty yards to run Affirmed found more and pushed his white blaze in front of his rival. Alydar tried to respond to this last-gasp challenge but he had given his all, and Affirmed won by a head. 'He really had to fight for that one,' said Cauthen later. The third horse Darby Creek Road was over thirteen lengths behind Alydar.

Affirmed and Alydar had earnt a joint place in Triple Crown lore: Affirmed had become the eleventh horse to win the Crown, and Alydar had been second in all three races, with the aggregate of winning distances in the three less than two lengths. For Gerald

Strine in the *Washington Post*, 'this was a race to be enjoyed and remembered, the end to a Triple Crown series that was without equal in terms of a two-horse rivalry.' And for Steve Cauthen, 'it was a real horse race, all right.'

By the time of their final meeting, in the Travers Stakes at Saratoga, Alydar had won the Arlington Classic by thirteen lengths and the Whitney Stakes by ten, and Affirmed had lifted the Jim Dandy Stakes. Steve Cauthen was sidelined, and Laffit Pincay replaced him on Affirmed. Going into the final turn Affirmed cut in on Alydar and caused him to stumble, and though Alydar tried to recover the ground lost in the incident he finished two lengths behind Affirmed. It came as no great surprise when Affirmed was disqualified and Alydar given the race. So the final tally after ten races was seven to Affirmed, three to Alydar.

Alydar suffered a setback while in training for yet another crack at Affirmed in the Marlboro Cup, and though he was able to run in 1979 he was not the horse he had once been. After breaking down for a second time he was retired to stud in Kentucky. Affirmed was beaten by the great four-year-old Seattle Slew in the Marlboro Cup and then had to be pulled up in the Jockey Club Gold Cup after Cauthen's saddle slipped, but in 1979 he went on to conquer fresh heights, and he added that season's Horse Of The Year title to the one he had taken in 1978.

Affirmed won seven of his nine races in 1979, notably a famous three-quarter-length victory over Spectacular Bid in the Jockey Club Gold Cup. By the time he was retired to Spendthrift Farm in Kentucky he had won $2,393,818 – the first horse to cross the two-million-dollar barrier – and been beaten only seven times in twenty-nine starts. But such statistics are less relevant than the memory of him in action. He went hell for leather and proved almost impossible to pass. For an appropriate summary of Affirmed's racing career we can do no better than the words his trainer Laz Barrera spoke to his owners Mr and Mrs Louis Wolfson as their horse shot out of the starting gate in the 1979 Jockey Club Gold Cup: 'When Affirmed breaks like that you can put the beans on the fire – you're gonna eat for sure.'

# ARD PATRICK, SCEPTRE AND ROCK SAND

*Eclipse Stakes*
*Sandown Park, 17 July 1903*

---

## Eclipse Stakes

Sandown Park
1¼ miles
17 July 1903

| | | |
|---|---|---|
| 1 Ard Patrick | O. Madden | 5–1 |
| 2 Sceptre | F. W. Hardy | 7–4 |
| 3 Rock Sand | J. H. Martin | 5–4 fav. |

*Also ran:* Duke of Westminster (4th), Oriole

5 ran

Winner owned by J. Gubbins, trained by S. Darling

*Distances:* neck, 3 lengths

*❛ The horse just outran the mare ❜*

'About the best thing in racing is when two good horses single themselves out from the rest of the field and have a long-drawn-out struggle,' wrote the trainer George Lambton in his famous book *Men and Horses I Have Known.* Many of the races in this book fit that description, but the race to which Lambton was specifically alluding – and a race long acclaimed as the greatest contest of the century's early years – was the 1903 Eclipse Stakes, which pitched the three-year-old Rock Sand against the year-older Ard Patrick and the legendary filly Sceptre, also aged four.

By 1903 the Eclipse Stakes, though less than two decades old, was firmly established as one of the key races of the calendar, the first occasion on which the top middle-distance three-year-olds could take on older horses. Many of the most famous names of turn-of-the-century racing had won the race since 1886; but rarely has any race attracted such a high-class field as the 1903 renewal, the £10,000 prize money for which made it hugely valuable by the standards of the day.

Sceptre, one of the greatest fillies in the history of the Turf, was bred by the Duke of Westminster and sold on his death to Bob Sievier, one of the most colourful characters of turn-of-the-century racing. His handling of Sceptre was characteristically bizarre. She had won two of her three races as a two-year-old when trained by Charles Morton, but when Morton went off to become private trainer to J. B. Joel at the end of the season, Sievier decided to train Sceptre himself, and for her three-year-old debut chose the Lincolnshire Handicap – though a 23-runner one-mile handicap was a highly unusual target for a filly with Classic possibilities! Sievier gambled in phenomenal amounts and expected to make a killing by running a filly of Sceptre's class in such a race, but she had been overworked by Sievier's assistant trainer and was beaten by the four-year-old St Maclou. She then went for the Classics, winning the Two Thousand Guineas in record time and adding the One Thousand two days later. Starting even-money favourite for the Derby, she could finish only fourth to Ard Patrick, but redeemed herself in the Oaks at 5–2. Later in the season she

won the St Leger to become the only horse ever to win four Classics outright. Despite Sceptre's successes, by the end of 1902 Sievier was feeling the pinch again, so he tried to sell his prize filly at the December Sales. When she failed to reach her reserve of 24,000 guineas he decided to train her for another attempt at the Lincoln, but this time she only managed fifth. She was then sold for £25,000 to William Bass and was moved to the stable of the great trainer Alec Taylor at Manton. In her first run in Bass's colours she won the Hardwicke Stakes at Royal Ascot before going for the Eclipse.

Ard Patrick had triumphed in the one Classic that had eluded Sceptre in 1902, beating the filly into fourth place in the Derby (though he had been third to her in the Two Thousand Guineas) and he had tuned up for the Sandown Park race with an easy victory in the Princess of Wales's Stakes at Newmarket. But it was the three-year-old Rock Sand who started favourite for the Eclipse, and with good reason: defeated only once as a two-year-old, he came to Sandown unbeaten at three, a Two Thousand Guineas and Derby winner.

Sceptre had not long been at Manton and Alec Taylor was not sure whether he yet had her right. Rock Sand had followed up his Derby victory with a triumph in the St James's Palace Stakes at Royal Ascot. Ard Patrick had been aimed at the Eclipse all season by his trainer Sam Darling, whose eye for detail in the horse's preparation included working his charge over the full ten-furlong course so that he would become accustomed to Sandown's bends and, to make assurance doubly sure, fitting flanges on the outer heels of Ard Patrick's shoes for the race to give him a better grip on the firm but slippery going.

George Lambton went to the paddock to inspect the runners: 'When I saw these three champions walking round the ring, much as I loved Rock Sand, and often as I had won money on him, I had to give him third place. A beautifully made horse and not by any means a small one, yet the other two were a pair of giants, both in performances and stature, and the old saying that a good big one will beat a good little one was borne irresistibly into my mind.' The bookmakers did not

Ard Patrick (left) holds off
Sceptre by a neck.

Trainer Sam Darling leads in Ard
Patrick.

share Lambton's view and Rock Sand (who carried nine stone four pounds) started the 5–4 favourite, with Sceptre (nine stone thirteen) at 7–4 and Ard Patrick (ten stone two) the least fancied of the trio at 5–1. The two other runners were unconsidered outsiders – this was a three-horse race.

And so it proved. The favourite Rock Sand was going easily enough as the runners negotiated the long turn into the straight, but with half a mile to go he was struggling, and his two older rivals drew away. Sceptre, ridden by Fred Hardy, took a slight lead and appeared to be holding on, but Otto Madden on Ard Patrick was timing his run to perfection. Halfway up the straight the two were running neck and neck as the crowd raised an almighty clamour. The yells were mainly for Sceptre, and indeed with two furlongs to race she seemed to be gaining the upper hand. Inside the final furlong, according to Lambton's account, 'Sceptre looked the winner, as she had drawn slightly ahead, but Madden was a jockey who knew exactly where the winning post was, and he nursed Ard Patrick beautifully for that last hundred yards, with the result that the horse just outran the mare and won by a neck.'

It had been a desperate struggle and one of the finest races ever seen, but the crowd, the great majority of whom idolized Sceptre,

was deeply disappointed that she had just failed and scarcely gave Ard Patrick the reception he deserved. And controversy followed about whether the result was a true reflection of the horses' merits. George Lambton thought Sceptre might have won had her new trainer had her longer and known enough about her to give her a more searching preparation, but Sam Darling unsurprisingly took the view that his charge was just the better horse.

Ard Patrick never ran again: the leg trouble which had plagued him earlier in his career recurred and he was retired to stud in Germany. Sceptre, none the worse for her exertions, won four more races that season, including the Champion Stakes at Newmarket. In the Jockey Club Stakes on the same course she beat Rock Sand by four lengths giving him seven pounds more than the weight-for-age-and-sex allowance, by which time Rock Sand had gone on to win the St Leger (and thus the Triple Crown). The following season he met Sceptre again in the Coronation Cup, when they were both beaten by Zinfandel in Rock Sand's only defeat as a four year old. In 1904 Sceptre was also beaten in the Ascot Gold Cup and in the Hardwicke Stakes – but at least she did not have to make another attempt at the Lincoln.

# BRIGADIER GERARD, MILL REEF AND MY SWALLOW

*Two Thousand Guineas*
*Newmarket, 1 May 1971*

Any race which brings together two outstanding horses running true to form is sure to be a great race. The 1971 Two Thousand Guineas brought together three. And if the debate about the relative merits of Brigadier Gerard and Mill Reef can still prolong delicious racing debate well into the early hours, the result of their one and only race against each other remains conclusive.

The early 1970s was a golden age for European Flat racing, for even as Nijinsky in 1970 was dominating the three-year-old scene by becoming the first colt to win the English Triple Crown since Bahram in 1935, three two-year-olds were proclaiming themselves racehorses of exceptional merit. Mill Reef, owned by Paul Mellon and trained by Ian Balding, had opened his account at Salisbury in May with an easy four-length victory over 9–2 on chance Fireside Chat and had proceeded to win the Coventry Stakes at Royal Ascot by eight lengths. He had then gone for the Prix Robert Papin at Maisons-Laffitte, one of France's top two-year-old races, where he had come up against the

brilliant and unbeaten My Swallow, trained in England by Paul Davey for David Robinson and ridden by Lester Piggott. Mill Reef had endured a terrible journey across the Channel and was not at his best, but still ran My Swallow to a short head. He then returned to winning form with a ten-length victory in very heavy going in the Gimcrack Stakes at York before taking the Imperial Stakes at Kempton Park and rounding off his juvenile career with a facile victory in Newmarket's Dewhurst Stakes. Meanwhile Brigadier Gerard had been making his own waves with an unbeaten two-year-old career consisting of four races: the Berkshire Stakes at Newbury (which he won at 100–7), the Champagne Stakes at Salisbury (13–8 on), the Washington Singer Stakes at Newbury (9–4 on) and the Middle Park Stakes at Newmarket, where he started at 9–2 and beat odds-on chance Mummy's Pet by three lengths.

On two-year-old form Mill Reef and My Swallow seemed to have the edge over Brigadier Gerard. Mill Reef's arguably excusable defeat in the Prix Robert Papin had

*Leaving the paddock for the clash of the three superstars: Mill Reef (Geoff Lewis).*

❜ *My God, did he pick up!* ❛

been his only failure in six races, and My Swallow had ended the 1970 season unbeaten in seven: in addition to his Maisons-Laffitte victory over Mill Reef he had won the Prix Morny, the Grand Criterium, the Prix Salamandre and the Prix du Bois as well as the Zetland Stakes at York and the Woodcote Stakes at Epsom. The Two-Year-Old Free Handicap, the official assessment of the merits of each year's young generation, rated My Swallow one pound superior to Mill Reef and two pounds superior to Brigadier Gerard.

My Swallow began his three-year-old career with victory in the Usher Stakes at Kempton Park, while Mill Reef strolled home in the Greenham Stakes at Newbury. Brigadier Gerard went to Newmarket for the Guineas without a previous outing, though his performances on the home gallops had inspired his connections (owner-breeder John Hislop, trainer Dick Hern and jockey Joe Mercer) with great confidence – which in Hislop's case was just as well, for shortly before the Guineas he had turned down an offer of £250,000 for the horse. One particu-

larly encouraging gallop a week before the race convinced those close to Brigadier Gerard that he was something out of the ordinary; but few were convinced that he could beat Mill Reef and My Swallow, and the betting reflected the widely held feeling that it would be a two-horse race: Mill Reef started 6–4 favourite, with My Swallow 2–1 and Brigadier Gerard 11–2. The other three runners were Minsky (15–2), a full brother to Nijinsky and winner of his two races that year in Ireland; Good Bond (16–1), winner of the Ascot Two Thousand Guineas Trial; and Indian Ruler (100–1), an impressive two-year-old winner at Newmarket but beaten by Good Bond at Ascot.

In the paddock before the race the massed spectators were bubbling with anticipation. All too rarely do such showdowns between the best horses actually come off, and the excitement was intense as the runners were led round. They presented a contrast in physique: My Swallow was a very tall and imposing bay colt, sporting a sheepskin noseband across his handsome white blaze. Brigadier Gerard, who had grown into as

*My Swallow (Frankie Durr).*

## Two Thousand Guineas

Newmarket
1 mile
1 May 1971

| | | |
|---|---|---|
| 1 Brigadier Gerard | J. Mercer | 11–2 |
| 2 Mill Reef | G. Lewis | 6–4 fav. |
| 3 My Swallow | F. Durr | 2–1 |

*Also ran:* Minsky (4th), Good Bond, Indian Ruler

6 ran

Winner owned by Mrs J. L. Hislop, trained by W. R. Hern

*Distances:* 3 lengths, ³/₄ length

*Brigadier Gerard (Joe Mercer).*

magnificent a three-year-old as you could wish to see, was cool and composed, which is more than could be said for Minsky: his coltish antics seemed to be upsetting Mill Reef, who started playing up and trying to get away from his lad. Mill Reef was a size smaller than his main rivals, but like them was superbly turned out and trained to the minute. For sheer quality Brigadier Gerard had to be the pick of the paddock. Both Mill Reef and Brigadier Gerard were ridden by their regular jockeys – Geoff Lewis and Joe Mercer respectively – while Frankie Durr was aboard My Swallow. The weather was warm and sunny, the day clear, the going on the firm side of good. The scene was truly set for a great race.

When the stalls opened My Swallow went straight into the lead from his berth on the outside of the field and made the early running, as was his custom. Mill Reef, drawn on the inside, tacked over to join him, with Brigadier Gerard two or three lengths in arrears and the remaining three runners soon beating a retreat. Durr continued to set a good

though not breakneck pace on My Swallow, and three furlongs out Mill Reef moved alongside, while behind them Mercer brought Brigadier Gerard over to the stands side to make his challenge. But the pair in front showed no signs of stopping, and most spectators still thought they were watching a two-horse race. Not for long, though. With two furlongs to go Mercer gave his mount one slap with the whip. It took Brigadier Gerard a few strides to get into top gear, but once he reached full speed the effect was devastating. 'My God, did he pick up!', reported the jockey of how, a furlong and a half out, Brigadier Gerard swept down into the Dip and past Mill Reef and My Swallow, racing together in the centre of the course. They had no response to this pulverizing burst of speed, and Brigadier Gerard charged up the hill to the winning post with Joe Mercer's whip swinging rhythmically on his right side. At the line he was three lengths clear. Mill Reef took second by three quarters of a length from My Swallow, with Minsky a distant fourth.

*The other two are well out of shot
as Brigadier Gerard scoots home.*

Brigadier Gerard had put up the most brilliant performance in the Two Thousand Guineas since Tudor Minstrel in 1947. Over the next eighteen months he established himself as one of the greatest horses ever: by the time he was retired to stud in the autumn of 1972 he had won seventeen of his eighteen races, including the King George VI and Queen Elizabeth stakes, the Eclipse Stakes, the Champion Stakes (twice), the Sussex Stakes and the Queen Elizabeth II Stakes (twice). After the Two Thousand Guineas Mill Reef was never beaten again, winning the Derby, the Eclipse, the King George and the Prix de l'Arc de Triomphe (see pages 102–3) in 1971 and the Prix Ganay and the

Coronation Cup the following year. The prospect of these two wonderful horses engaging in a rematch in the inaugural running of the Benson and Hedges Gold Cup at York in August 1972 whipped the British racing public into a frenzy, but two disappointments ensued: Mill Reef pulled a muscle in training and could not run, and in the race itself Brigadier Gerard suffered his only defeat when going down by three lengths to that year's Derby winner Roberto.

Arguments still rage about whether Brigadier Gerard or Mill Reef was the better horse but on 1 May 1971 there was no doubt which was the greater.

# QUASHED AND OMAHA

*Gold Cup*
*Ascot, 18 June 1936*

*Quashed (near side) just refuses to give in as Omaha comes at her.*

❜ To see Quashed and Omaha battle out the finish of the Ascot Gold Cup took years off a man's life ❛

Omaha and Quashed. Like Ferdinand and Alysheba, Grundy and Bustino, Arkle and Mill House, Monksfield and Sea Pigeon, their names will be linked for ever in the annals of horse racing. For the head-to-head struggle between these two four-year-olds – he winner of the American Triple Crown, she winner of the Oaks – in the 1936 Ascot Gold Cup is still held by many pundits to be the most exciting Flat race run in Britain this century.

Omaha had been the best three-year-old in the USA in 1935, taking the Triple Crown. But he had gone lame later that summer and his owner William Woodward, one of the most respected and influential figures on the American and British Turf in the years between the wars, sent him early in 1936 to continue his racing career with Captain Cecil Boyd-Rochfort in Newmarket. The target was the Ascot Gold Cup, in those days one of the most sought-after prizes of the

season, and Omaha, a large and powerful chestnut, seemed in many ways ideally suited for the race. But Ascot is a right-handed course and presented Omaha with a very different proposition from the left-handed American tracks on which he had always run previously, so in order to get him used to running in the 'wrong' direction his first two races in England were round the right-hand turns of Kempton Park: he started at 5–4 on in the Victor Wild Stakes early in May 1936 and won easily, then followed up with a neck victory in the Queen's Plate less than three weeks before his date at Ascot.

In contrast to her rival, Quashed – owned by Lord Stanley and trained by Colledge Leader – was a lithe and leggy filly, who in her early days had been thought by her breeder a possible Grand National candidate! A promising two-year-old career put paid to any such notions, and by the summer of 1935 she had done well enough to earn her place in the Oaks at Epsom: despite starting an unconsidered outsider at 33–1, she put in a rousing finish to win the Classic by a short head, then underwent a taxing campaign (including running third in the Cesarewitch carrying eight stone nine pounds) before winding up her season with an impressive victory in the Jockey Club Cup over two and a quarter miles at Newmarket. She was clearly an out-and-out stayer and remarkably tough, and she showed herself in good trim for the Gold Cup by winning her first two races of the 1936 season – the Great Metropolitan Handicap at Epsom and the Ormonde Stakes at Chester.

The Ascot going was soft for the third day of the Royal meeting, Gold Cup Day, and the weather misty. As usual there was a vast crowd, and the press of people craning to get a look at the American challenger seemed to cause Omaha to sweat profusely, which he had not done on a racecourse before. Nevertheless he started a firm favourite at 11–8, with Quashed at 3–1. Valerius, winner of the Yorkshire Cup, was third favourite at 9–1, and the other six runners – who included three challengers from France – attracted little attention in the betting ring.

Omaha was ridden by Rufus Beasley, who had partnered him in his two previous races in Britain, and Quashed by Richard Perryman. Neither jockey was in a hurry to force the issue in the early part of the race: the pace was made first by the French horse Chaudiere and then by Buckleigh. As the runners swung into the straight with less than three furlongs to go Buckleigh still held the lead, but now Quashed had gone past Chaudiere into second, with another French raider Bokbul fourth and Omaha moving up gradually from the rear and at this stage looking like the winner. Bokbul came wide round the bend and Omaha, about to make his move on the stands side, was carried out with him, while on the inside Quashed had taken up the running from Buckleigh. But Omaha was still on the bridle and as he set off after the filly he seemed sure to catch her. With just over a furlong to go he was practically level and still looked to have more in hand, but Quashed kept staying on, and the pair raced into the final two hundred yards

locked together. Omaha then seemed to head the filly but Quashed would not hear of defeat, and rallied with the utmost gameness. Beasley went for his whip but dropped it, and Omaha started to hang left under pressure. The two flashed past the post together, and no one in the stands could say for sure which had won. The judge gave it to Quashed, by a short head: the first filly to win the Gold Cup this century.

As is so often the case after a very close contest, every detail was re-examined to see if affairs might have turned out differently under different circumstances. If Beasley had not lost his whip in those last desperate moments would Omaha have run straight and not forfeited precious ground? Had the jockey been allowed to follow his own inclination and save Omaha for one late burst, rather than attacking the filly early in the straight (as owner William Woodward had insisted) would not that have put Quashed's undoubted stamina at less of a premium? Much more sensationally, could Omaha's uncharacteristic sweating up before the race have been caused – as his owner thought – by the attentions of the Squirt Gang, who would squirt burning acid at a hot favourite before a race in order to upset it into performing badly? Thirteen years later Woodward wrote to trainer Boyd-Rochfort from the USA: 'I am confident that some underworld fellow sprayed Omaha with "high-life". They do this at a distance of three or four feet by using little so-called guns which look like a fountain pen. They use these things in holding up banks in this country.'

Neither horse was as good again, though Quashed won the Jockey Club Cup later in 1936 from a single opponent and was third to Precipitation in the Gold Cup in 1937. Omaha ran only a fortnight after his heroic performance at Ascot, in the Princess of Wales's Stakes at Newmarket: again he proved excitable, refusing for several minutes to line up to face the starter, and when the race eventually got under way he was beaten a neck. He never ran again.

In his book *Sods I Have Cut on the Turf* the ex-jockey Jack Leach wrote: 'to see Quashed and Omaha battle out the finish of the Ascot Gold Cup took years off a man's life, though it was well worth it.'

## Gold Cup

Ascot
2½ miles
18 June 1936

| 1 | Quashed | R. Perryman | 3–1 |
| 2 | Omaha | P. Beasley | 11–8 fav. |
| 3 | Bokbul | C. Elliott | 100–6 |

*Also ran:* Robin Goodfellow (4th), Samos II, Valerius, Patriot King, Buckleigh, Chaudiere

9 ran

Winner owned by Lord Stanley, trained by C. Leader

*Distances:* short head, 5 lengths

# ARKLE AND MILL HOUSE

*Cheltenham Gold Cup*
*Cheltenham, 7 March 1964*

The 1964 Cheltenham Gold Cup produced such a famous race that there was even a song recorded about it. Dominic Behan's rousing ballad *Arkle* lampoons the English notions of the invincibility of Mill House, revels in how they were dashed by the brilliance of Arkle, then satirizes the excuses which the English sought for their hero's defeat.

For this was the day of reckoning, the showdown between Arkle and Mill House which brought together two young horses already acknowledged to be among the finest performers in the history of steeplechasing, one trained in England and one in Ireland and each loyally championed by supporters who would not hear of defeat. This race would sort out who was the king.

In the one corner was 'the Big Horse'. Mill House was a huge gelding trained by Fulke Walwyn at Lambourn and had won the Gold Cup the year before at the tender age of six – the youngest horse to do so since Golden Miller in 1932. Bred in Ireland and bought for a substantial sum by advertising executive Bill Gollings, Mill House had been trained by Syd Dale on arriving in England and on his British debut had suffered the indignity of falling at the first flight of hurdles. After two more hurdle races (one of which he won) he was sent chasing, and soon showed himself a horse of immense promise. In the 1962–3 season, by the beginning of which he had been moved to Fulke Walwyn, he had won four of his five races; in the other he had blundered at the last fence at Kempton Park and been pipped by half a length by the good chaser King's Nephew. The young Mill House was a somewhat gauche jumper, but as he learned his business he developed into a formidable chaser: when his giant stride and his awe-inspiring fencing were in tune he looked in a different league from his contemporaries, and after his twelve-length Gold Cup victory over Fortria in March 1963 he was being hailed as the greatest steeplechaser since Golden Miller. With plenty of time on his side, Mill House was confidently expected to outstrip even The Miller's achievements. In the 1964 Gold Cup he would be ridden by Willie Robinson, as he had been in all his races since coming to Fulke Walwyn's stable. Mill

House would not fail for want of human expertise, and to chasing fans in Britain he seemed invincible.

There was as much confidence in the other corner. Arkle was also a seven-year-old, trained in Ireland by Tom Dreaper and ridden at Cheltenham by his regular partner Pat Taaffe. Arkle too was Irish-bred, and had been bought as a three-year-old for 1150 guineas by Anne, Duchess of Westminster. For the next year of his life he was left to mature on the Duchess's Cheshire estate, returning to Ireland to be trained by Tom Dreaper in August 1961. On his arrival at Dreaper's stable at Killsallaghan there was little hint of the brilliance which was to illuminate the steeplechasing scene a few short years later: head lad Paddy Murphy reported that 'he looked the worst of all the four-year-olds who arrived that season. He was unfurnished. And he moved bad.' Arkle did not move bad for long. After finishing unplaced in two National Hunt Flat races, he started at 20–1 for the Bective Novice Hurdle at Navan on 20 January 1962 and won. In his next race – a hurdle at Naas – he was ridden for the first time by Pat Taaffe, and obliged at 2–1. He then ran unplaced and fourth in two more handicap hurdles, and that was enough for his first term.

The following season life started to get serious. After two wins over hurdles he had his first run in a steeplechase on 17 November 1962 in the Honeybourne Chase at Cheltenham. Favourite at 11–8, Arkle won this two-and-a-half-mile race with eye-catching ease by twenty lengths. Having won a two-mile chase at Leopardstown in February 1963 he returned to Cheltenham for the Broadway Chase at the Festival meeting: again he won with ridiculous ease by twenty lengths. Two days later Mill House won his Gold Cup, and the racing world licked its lips in anticipation of the first meeting between these two young giants.

It came in the Hennessy Gold Cup at Newbury on 30 November 1963. Both horses were unbeaten since their Cheltenham races – Mill House in just one race late the previous season, Arkle in four, two of which were warm-up races for Newbury. Under the terms of the handicap Mill House carried five pounds more than the Dreaper horse

*This is the champion!*

but started 15–8 favourite; Arkle was 5–2. Mill House handed Arkle a comprehensive beating, jumping with great verve and running his rivals ragged. Arkle was third, the first time he had experienced defeat over fences, but he had slipped on landing over the third last fence (the final open ditch), and the Arkle supporters held the result to be inconclusive. To the Mill House camp the Arkle slip was an excuse; to the Arkle, it was an explanation, and their hero would not slip up – literally or figuratively – again.

Between Newbury and Cheltenham neither horse did anything to disabuse his supporters of the complete conviction that their hero would emerge triumphant in the Gold Cup. Mill House won the King George VI Chase at Kempton Park and the Gainsborough Chase at Sandown Park; Arkle strode to victory in three chases in Ireland.

Only two other horses had the impertinence to take on the big rivals at Cheltenham. Pas Seul had been an exceptional steeplechaser and had won the Gold Cup in 1960 but now, at the age of eleven, was a shadow of his former self, while King's Nephew had beaten Mill House the previous season but was surely out of his depth in this company, as evidenced by the starting prices: 13–8 on Mill House, 7–4 Arkle, 20–1 King's Nephew, 50–1 Pas Seul.

As this small but highly select field paraded in the paddock – Mill House massive but nimble, Arkle with a less impressive physique but a bundle of energy and clearly trained to the minute – the mood of anticipation was almost tangible. This race had been so eagerly awaited, and its outcome debated so late into the night, that it seemed almost too good to be true that it was actually taking place at all. Even the weather wanted to salute the occasion, and as the runners reached the start (which in those days was on a spur of the Cheltenham course to the rear of the grandstand) a brief snowstorm blew across the track from the neighbouring Cleeve Hill to interrupt a cold but sunny Saturday afternoon.

Soon the four horses were on their way, Mill House going straight into the lead and soaring over the first fence. He flew over the second – an open ditch – and headed out into the country. Arkle was taking his fences more economically but pulling very hard, and it was as much as Pat Taaffe could do to keep him behind the leader. He hit the fence at the top of the hill and fell back a little, to be passed momentarily by Pas Seul, but Arkle was not a horse who enjoyed restraint and as the quartet came down the hill for the first time he had pulled his way back into second place.

As they came past the stands Mill House continued to bowl along in the lead, and

*Crossing his forelegs in characteristic fashion, Arkle leaves Mill House behind at the last fence.*

going out for the second time Robinson decided to step up the pace. Arkle was having no difficulty staying within striking distance and Taaffe was in no hurry, and by the water jump on the second circuit – the fourteenth of the twenty-one obstacles in the race – Pas Seul and King's Nephew had fallen away. The title-holder Mill House was trying to gallop the aspirant into the ground, but Arkle was the horse with the speed, and at each fence Robinson had to try to shake off the challenge with the flamboyance of his partner's jumping. Going to the fifteenth Mill House seemed for a second to have the legs of Arkle: he went five lengths clear and Arkle fiddled his jump. But at the next Arkle threw a brilliant leap, and at the final open ditch he was closing.

Now they were climbing the hill, and Mill House was not losing his opponent. As they turned towards the third last it looked to Arkle's supporters in the crowd as if their horse had the English-trained runner for the taking, and the Irish bellowed their encouragement to Pat Taaffe, the best part of a mile away. At the third last Mill House was still two lengths clear, and he put in a superb jump. But Arkle was unimpressed, and nonchalantly swung along in the Big Horse's wake as the two came down the hill at a furious pace.

At the second last Mill House had the inside berth and touched down fractionally in front, but Taaffe was clearly just biding his time, and they swung into the straight to make the short run to the final fence. 'Now they're rounding the home turn,' shouted BBC commentator Peter O'Sullevan, 'and this is it!' Up went Robinson's arm; down came his whip. It was the moment of truth.

Now Taaffe shook the reins and asked Arkle to go on and win his race, and in a matter of strides the argument was settled, as Arkle swept past his rival and skipped over the final jump two lengths to the good. For a moment Mill House, his head doggedly stuck out, seemed to rally. He got back to within a length, but Taaffe kept pushing Arkle out and the issue was put beyond debate. 'This is the champion!', cried Peter O'Sullevan as Arkle scampered up the hill to victory with Mill House, until a few moments ago hailed as the greatest chaser

since Golden Miller, toiling in his wake. The winning margin was five lengths.

The Mill House camp was shell-shocked: 'I can still hardly believe that any horse breathing could have done what Arkle did to him,' said Fulke Walwyn afterwards, and although there was some clutching at straws by the big horse's supporters, it was generally recognized that not only had Arkle proved his complete superiority over Mill House, he had shown himself arguably the finest chaser ever. His performances over the next three years effectively removed the qualifying 'arguably' from that assessment. He met Mill House three more times, in the Hennessy Gold Cup the following December and in 1965 in the Cheltenham Gold Cup and the Gallaher Gold Cup (see pages 84–5): each time his superiority increased.

By the time his career came to its untimely end after he had broken a pedal bone in his hoof in the King George VI Chase at Kempton Park on 27 December 1966 Arkle had convinced all but a few diehard Golden Miller fans of his right to be hailed as the greatest steeplechaser of all – and marvellous as Desert Orchid's achievements have been, no judge of form seriously puts the great grey horse in the same league as Tom Dreaper's champion. Arkle was beaten only four times in twenty-six steeplechases, and his victories included three Cheltenham Gold Cups, two Hennessy Gold Cups (on both occasions carrying a handicap weight of twelve stone seven pounds), the King George VI Chase, the Whitbread Gold Cup (twelve stone seven pounds) and the Irish Grand National (twelve stone). So far above his fellows was he that the rules of racing in Ireland were amended to allow for the framing of two handicaps when Arkle was entered – one to include him, the other to be constructed without him so that if he did not run the lesser mortals could be handicapped according to their merits and not just lumped together way below Arkle.

He was the greatest. But as a single occasion, none of his subsequent achievements matched that sunny blizzardy Saturday in March 1964, when Arkle was crowned king. In the pubs of Ireland that race would be talked about – and sung about – for ever.

---

**Cheltenham Gold Cup**

Cheltenham
3 miles 2 furlongs 130 yards
7 March 1964

| 1 | Arkle | P. Taaffe | 7–4 |
| 2 | Mill House | G. W. Robinson | 8–13 fav. |
| 3 | King's Nephew | S. Mellor | 20–1 |

*Also ran:* Pas Seul (4th)

Winner owned by Anne, Duchess of Westminster, trained by T. W. Dreaper

*Distances:* 5 lengths, 25 lengths

# SUNDAY SILENCE AND EASY GOER

*Breeders' Cup Classic*
*Gulfstream Park, 4 November 1989*

*Sunday Silence (yellow cap) looms out of the darkness with Easy Goer (red cap) getting ever nearer...*

It was coming on dark when the eight runners for the Breeders' Cup Classic 1989 were taken down to the ten-furlong start at Gulfstream Park, Florida, at the end of a Breeders' Cup afternoon which had already seen brilliant performances – from Bayakoa in the Distaff, from Steinlen in the Mile, and from Prized and Sierra Roberta in the Turf. Although the Classic was the final event of the seven-race programme, no one was leaving the course to make a quick get-away. Floodlights bathed the track, but this was a race which would itself illuminate the deepest dusk. It was Easy Goer against Sunday Silence.

Their previous meetings had been in the three legs of the Triple Crown, and although by Breeders' Cup day their rivalry looked set to match that of Affirmed and Alydar a decade before (see pages 16–17), they had not met as two-year-olds. Alydar, second to Affirmed in all three Triple Crown races, had an interest in this new bout, for he was the sire of Easy Goer. Trained by Shug McGaughey for Ogden Phipps, Easy Goer had had six runs as a two-year-old, winning four times and finishing runner-up twice. Sunday Silence was trained in California by Charlie Whittingham and owned by a triumvirate which consisted of Arthur B. Hancock, Dr Ernest Gaillard and Whittingham himself, now seventy-six and one of the greatest trainers in American racing history. Sunday Silence won one of his three juvenile races

*... and at the wire Sunday Silence has it by a neck.*

❝ *I still think I have the best horse and they think they have the best horse* ❞

and finished second in the others.

By the time of their first meeting in the Kentucky Derby both colts were unbeaten as three-year-olds with three wins apiece – which for Easy Goer included the Wood Memorial and the Whitney, and for Sunday Silence the Santa Anita Derby by eleven lengths. At Churchill Downs it was Sunday Silence who drew first blood with a two-and-a-half-length victory. His Derby win was held by some to be a fluke, but he confirmed the form in the second leg two weeks later, beating Easy Goer – on whom Pat Day rode a widely criticized race – by a nose in the third fastest Preakness yet. In the Belmont Stakes

over a mile and a half it was a different story as Easy Goer smashed his rival's Triple Crown pretensions with a stunning eight-length victory. After that they went their separate ways. Easy Goer maintained his progress to register decisive wins in four Grade One events, including a four-length beating of Cryptoclearance in the Jockey Club Gold Cup at Belmont Park in October; Sunday Silence had only two races between the Belmont Stakes and the Classic, suffering a shock defeat in the Swaps Stakes before redeeming himself with a six-length hammering of seven opponents in the Super Derby at Louisiana Downs.

*In a quieter moment, Charlie Whittingham tries to cheer up Sunday Silence.*

**Breeders' Cup Classic**

Gulfstream Park
1¼ miles
4 November 1989

| 1 Sunday Silence | C. McCarron | 2–1 |
| 2 Easy Goer | P. Day | 1–2 fav. |
| 3 Blushing John | A. Cordero | 22–1 |

*Also ran:* Present Value (4th),
Cryptoclearance, Slew City Slew, Western
Playboy, Mi Selecto

8 ran

Winner owned by E. Gaillard, A. Hancock III
and C. Whittingham, trained by C.
Whittingham

*Distances:* neck, 1 length

So as night fell on Gulfstream Park here was a true showdown between two exceptional three-year-old colts, and the tension in the 50,000-strong crowd rose as the gloom descended and the lights came on. Easy Goer had run sixteen races and Sunday Silence eleven, and neither had ever finished out of the first two. Easy Goer was ridden by his regular jockey Pat Day. Chris McCarron was on Sunday Silence for the first time.

There were six other horses in the race. Western Playboy was fresh from a seventeen-length victory in the Pennsylvania Derby; Cryptoclearance had won twelve races worth over $3 million but was well held by Easy Goer on Jockey Club Gold Cup form; Blushing John had won the French equivalent of the Two Thousand Guineas when trained in France by François Boutin and had won five races in the USA in 1989. The remaining three were Present Value, Slew City Slew and Mi Selecto. At the start the pari-mutuel price of Easy Goer was 2–1 on. Sunday Silence was 2–1 against. The next in the betting was Western Playboy at 17–1.

It was the rank outsider Slew City Slew who made the early running, with Sunday Silence waiting just off the pace and moving well within himself. Easy Goer had been slow out of the gate and started to make up the leeway down the back stretch, but when McCarron started to move Sunday Silence into a position to challenge for the lead coming to the final turn, Day – who had his great rival firmly in his sights – did not make an immediate move to go with them, and lost valuable ground. Easy Goer then faltered again for a moment on entering the home stretch as Day asked him to change his legs for his final surge. So Sunday Silence had first run, and the race was well and truly on. The dark bay Sunday Silence, his white-blazed head sporting a green sheepskin noseband, had the rails and was hammering down the stretch for all he was worth, with Chris McCarron in the yellow and grey silks applying the whip with his left hand. But once headed for home the big chestnut Easy Goer started to apply his ground-devouring stride, and with Pat Day in Ogden Phipps's familiar black, cherry red cap crouched deep into the horse's flowing mane he seemed like some luminescent mythical beast. Up the stretch he charged, head stuck out determinedly, but Sunday Silence had put in too much to throw it away now, and although Easy Goer was finishing like a train and catching the leader all the way, Sunday Silence was too good a horse to cave in, and at the wire was still a neck in front. Blushing John was only a length back in third, and it was nearly ten more lengths back to the fourth horse, Present Value.

Sunday Silence had shown greater speed when it was most needed on the home turn, and the consensus of opinion after this mammoth race was that he might always have the edge at distances up to ten furlongs, while the less nimble Easy Goer would be seen to best effect at longer distances. But the race had been about courage and determination as well as tactics, and the later comment of Whittingham's assistant trainer Rodney Rash pointed to a key reason for their colt's victory: 'This is one fightin' son of a gun.'

It is typical of the competitiveness of American racing at the highest level that an immediate reaction to the Classic was to look forward to the next clash between these two giants, and Easy Goer's trainer Shug McGaughey summed up the essence of such head-on confrontations: 'I still think I have the best horse and they think they have the best horse.'

# GOLDEN MILLER AND THOMOND II

*Cheltenham Gold Cup*
*Cheltenham, 15 March 1935*

*Golden Miller is led out.*

B y the time of the 1935 Cheltenham Gold Cup there was no doubt that Golden Miller was the most remarkable chaser who had ever run. He had already won the Gold Cup three times, and in 1934 he had become the first (and to date the only) horse to have won the Cheltenham Gold Cup and the Grand National in the same season.

Golden Miller was trained by Basil Briscoe, who had bought him as an unseen three-year-old from Ireland. When the horse arrived at Briscoe's yard he scarcely seemed worth even the £500 paid for him – the trainer likened him to a carthorse – and his first racecourse appearance gave little hint of what was to come: he was unplaced in a two-mile hurdle at Southwell worth £58. But with experience he started to show his true ability, and by the time he was sold for £6000 to Dorothy Paget he had won two hurdle races and been beaten a head on his chasing debut at Newbury. Miss Paget, daughter of Lord Queensborough, was the greatest eccentric the racing world in Britain has seen: vehemently averse to the company of men and – when not at the races – a recluse in her house in Chalfont St Giles, she

raced and wagered on a huge scale and owned many notable horses, of which 'The Miller' was the greatest.

Golden Miller first ran in the Cheltenham Gold Cup during his second season of competition, taking the 1932 race at the tender age of five: no horse so young has won the race since. The following season he won all five of his chases (including a second Gold Cup, in which he beat Jock Whitney's Thomond II by ten lengths) before an ill-fated attempt at the Grand National, which in those days was worth more than ten times the value of the Gold Cup and completely dominated the steeplechasing season: Golden Miller unseated his rider Ted Leader on the second circuit. In the 1933–4 season he won three of his five races, including a third Gold Cup and the Grand National, in which he drew away from Delaneige and Thomond (who was conceding him two pounds) to score easily.

The aim for the next season was to bring off the double again, and all went according to plan as Golden Miller registered four chase victories before heading for the Cheltenham prize. The Gold Cup was expected to prove little more than a warm-up for the

> ❦ *When we are old we can sit back in our chairs and tell them that we did ride at least one day of our lives!* ❧

National, as Thomond, though entered for the race, was going to run in the two-mile Coventry Cup at Cheltenham instead. Accordingly Basil Briscoe had not brought Golden Miller to peak fitness for the Gold Cup, and was horrified to learn only two days before it that Jock Whitney had changed his mind and decided to ask Thomond to take on The Miller after all. Thomond had beaten Briscoe's horse at Kempton Park the previous season when in receipt of seven pounds and could be guaranteed to give Golden Miller a hard race: at a stroke the Gold Cup had been transformed from a Liverpool warm-up into a duel between the two best chasers of the age. In vain did Briscoe try to have Jock Whitney revert to his original plan: Thomond would race against Golden Miller. The confrontation produced one of the finest steeplechases ever run.

Three other horses were in the line-up. Kellsboro Jack, third in the race the previous year and winner of the Grand National in 1933, was little behind the big two in terms of ability, though he started at 100–7, with Golden Miller at 2–1 on favourite and Thomond at 5–2. Avenger and Southern Hero (who had beaten Golden Miller in a handicap the previous year) both started at 20–1. It was a field of the highest quality.

The going was firm, which favoured Thomond over Golden Miller, and the weather sunny – which is more than could be said for the mood of Dorothy Paget when she flew in from Germany shortly before the race to learn that her supposed certainty was now facing one of the toughest races of his life. To add to the problems brought on by the going, the lack of peak fitness, and – most of all – the presence of Thomond, Golden

*At the last fence, Golden Miller (near side) and Thomond II are stride for stride.*

**Cheltenham Gold Cup**

Cheltenham
3¼ miles
14 March 1935

| 1 | Golden Miller | G. Wilson | 1–2 fav. |
| 2 | Thomond II | W. Speck | 5–2 |
| 3 | Kellsboro Jack | D. Morgan | 100–7 |

*Also ran:* Avenger (4th), Southern Hero

Winner owned by Miss D. Paget, trained by
B. Briscoe

*Distances:* ¾ length, 5 lengths

Miller faced a further impediment in the
condition of his rider Gerry Wilson, who had
sustained an arm injury in a fall a few days
earlier and was still in considerable pain. But
this was going to be some race, and huge
numbers converged on Cheltenham, block-
ing the roads with traffic, cramming the
trains to capacity, jamming the turnstiles
and forcing their way through the hedges
which surrounded the course.

The race did not disappoint them. Southern Hero set a strong gallop but the field
stayed close together, with Avenger taking
second place ahead of Golden Miller and
Thomond, and Kellsboro Jack bringing up
the rear. The pace increased approaching
the third last fence and Southern Hero cried
enough, allowing Golden Miller and Thomond to come through to dispute the lead at
a tremendous pace, with Kellsboro Jack
making ground behind them. Going for the
second last the race lay between the leading
two, with Wilson pushing along on the big,
long-striding Golden Miller providing a stark
contrast to Billy Speck hugging the inside
rail on Thomond, a much smaller horse
whose tearaway energy needed nurturing
and then unleashing. They jumped the
second last together, but Golden Miller's
stride began to assert his superiority as they
made for the last and he went half a length
up. Speck would not give in; going for his
whip, he threw Thomond into the last to
such effect that the two horses came away
from the fence all but level. As they set off
stride for stride up the notorious Cheltenham hill, neither giving an inch, the crowd
was yelling wildly: gradually Golden Miller
took a slight advantage and, try as he might,
Thomond could not reclaim the deficit. Golden Miller won by three quarters of a length,
with Kellsboro Jack five lengths further back
in third.

Golden Miller won the race for a fifth time
in 1936; but by that time there had been a
sad postscript to the 1935 race. For Billy
Speck, whose inspired riding of Thomond
had almost brought about Golden Miller's
defeat in the race in which he was then
invincible, was killed at Cheltenham a few
weeks later. His untimely death adds great
poignancy to the toast which Speck was
reported to have made to his victorious rival
Gerry Wilson as they drank champagne after
this momentous contest: 'It was a grand race,
mate. And don't forget, when we are old we
can sit back in our chairs and tell them that
we did ride at least one day of our lives!'

# MONKSFIELD AND SEA PIGEON

*Champion Hurdle*
*Cheltenham, 14 March 1979*

*Sea Pigeon (red sleeves) has a slight advantage taking off at the last flight...*

**❛ He took all I gave him and did not squirm from it ❜**

For three successive years Monksfield and Sea Pigeon came together to the last flight in the Champion Hurdle having beaten off their opponents. In 1978 it was Monksfield who powered up the hill to a two-length victory. Two years later Sea Pigeon found the extra speed to beat his rival by seven lengths. But in 1979 they were separated by less than a length in the most gripping finale the Champion Hurdle has ever seen.

Monskfield was trained in Ireland by Des McDonogh. Unusually for a mature hurdler, he was an entire horse, not a gelding, but his racing career gave the lie to the notion that entires lack resolution as they get older: not this one, anyway, for even before his dour struggle with Sea Pigeon in the 1979 Champion Hurdle he had shown himself a horse of quite remarkable courage. Narrowly beaten in the 1976 Daily Express Triumph Hurdle, the season's top race for four-year-old hurdlers, he had run the great Night Nurse to two lengths in the Champion Hurdle in 1977 and then pushed the same horse to a dead heat in the Templegate Hurdle at Liverpool less than three weeks later. In 1978 his turn in the Champion arrived as he came away from Night Nurse at the second last hurdle and then held off Sea Pigeon, who before the final flight had seemed to be cruising.

Sea Pigeon himself had been a good-class horse on the Flat, winning the Duke of Edinburgh Stakes at Ascot on his only outing as a two-year-old and finishing seventh in the Derby behind Morston. Though he continued to run on the Flat, taking the Chester Cup twice and (later in 1979) the Ebor Handicap, he became a top-class hurdler, winning the Scottish Champion Hurdle in 1977 and 1978.

Controversy and rumour coloured the prelude to the 1979 Champion. Tommy Kinane, who had won the race on Monksfield in 1978, was replaced by Dessie Hughes

after Kinane's riding of the horse in the Erin Foods Champion Hurdle at Leopardstown had come in for some criticism, and the aggrieved jockey did not hide his feelings. There were the usual pre-big race rumours about the well-being of the main contestants: Sea Pigeon, it was said, had been bursting blood vessels and was not properly fit; and two days before the race Monksfield was reported as being lame and a doubtful runner. Lame he certainly was not, as was clearly apparent when he undertook an exercise gallop over a mile and three quarters on the very morning of the race – a highly unorthodox preparation.

Sea Pigeon was ridden by Jonjo O'Neill and had been ante-post favourite, but his price drifted from 7–2 to 6–1 as the Cheltenham going became ever heavier, for as a horse with flat-race speed he would not be suited by bottomless conditions. Monksfield was backed down to 9–4 favourite in a field of ten runners, among them Bird's Nest,

*... but Monksfield leaps on to level terms...*

*... and they set off up the hill together.*

contesting the race for the fourth time (he had been second to Night Nurse in 1976), Beacon Light (who had run in the race twice before), and three younger horses of great promise – Kybo, a well-backed second favourite, Connaught Ranger and Major Thompson.

The Champion Hurdle was run on the second day of the Festival meeting, and by the time of the race the ground had become exceedingly heavy, so most of the principals were kept to the outside, away from the worst of the going. Monksfield led at every flight, and racing down the hill towards the second last was being closely pursued by Beacon Light, Kybo and Sea Pigeon. Kybo, going ominously well, moved smoothly up to the leader at the second last but misjudged the jump and took a crashing fall, leaving Sea Pigeon as the only danger to a repeat win for the 1978 champion. Sea Pigeon, on the inside, was apparently cruising to victory as the two came to the last, O'Neill not yet having asked his mount a serious question and Hughes already giving the ultra-game Monksfield a taste of the whip. The pair touched down together, then Sea Pigeon went into a narrow lead and looked set for a cheeky win – but Monksfield, his head stuck out in characteristically courageous fashion, simply would not give best, and in the last few desperate strides inched his way back in front. At the line he had won by three quarters of a length.

It had been a classic encounter and it set Cheltenham buzzing, for both horses had shown tremendous resolution and neither really deserved to lose. If either was scarred by such a gruelling finish in those appalling conditions they showed no sign of it a year later, as yet again they came to the last hurdle together. This time the Champion was run on the opening day of the Festival meeting so the going was not so bad, and the distance of the race had been shortened to two miles: both alterations were in Sea Pigeon's favour, and he duly took advantage. By the time he won his second title, bounding away from Pollardstown in 1981, Monksfield had been retired to stud, where he died in 1989.

The enduring memory of Monksfield at Cheltenham, where he ran in big Festival races for five successive seasons and never finished lower than second, is of his courage: head down and thrust forward, he scurried up the hill as if the Hounds of Hell were only a length adrift. Never has racing seen such a battler, as jockey Dessie Hughes acknowledged: 'He took all I gave him and did not squirm from it.'

# SEABISCUIT AND WAR ADMIRAL

*Pimlico Special*
*Pimlico, 1 November 1938*

*Seabiscuit pulls clear of War Admiral . . .*

❝ *This is down my alley* ❞

The fame of the match between Sea-biscuit and War Admiral, run on the first day of the 1938 autumn meeting at Pimlico, Baltimore, will endure as long as horse racing continues to exert its fascination. For this was a a horse race pure and simple – a head-to-head contest, with no other runners to provide distractions or excuses, between the two outstanding American horses of the era, horses from different generations, from opposite ends of their vast country and with starkly contrasting backgrounds and styles of running. The winner would take all.

War Admiral was the aristocrat. A son of Man O' War, he had been unbeaten the previous season, winning the Triple Crown and taking the Horse of the Year title. Owned like his sire by Samuel Doyle Riddle, he had been campaigned carefully by trainer George Conway and came to Pimlico the winner of eighteen of his twenty-two races, victories together worth nearly $264,000.

By any standards he was a champion.

Seabiscuit, owned by Charles S. Howard and trained in California by Tom Smith, had come up the hard way. Though himself a grandson of Man O' War (his sire was Hard Tack), it had taken him eighteen races as a two-year-old to get as far as winning one small event and he had been running in claimers. Yet despite having to travel all over the country to earn his corn he had gradually developed into a top-class horse, and in 1937 had been the leading money-winner in the USA. By the time he eventually met War Admiral he had earned $325,480, winning thirty-one of his eighty-three races.

American owners tended then (as now) to embrace the notion – somewhat rare in the higher echelons of European racing – that the best racehorses should compete with each other if their true merit is to be assessed properly, and by the beginning of the 1938 season the prospect of a showdown between the four-year-old War Admiral

*... and is led in by owner Charles S. Howard.*

and the five-year-old Seabiscuit (who had never met) gripped the American racing world.

It was Alfred Gwynne Vanderbilt who, having acquired a controlling interest in the Pimlico racetrack, finally brought the long-awaited match to fruition, negotiating an arrangement with Riddle and Howard that the race would be run over nine and a half furlongs on 1 November, both horses to carry 120 pounds. The small print included Riddle's demand that Pimlico's starter James F. Milton, whom he did not hold in high regard, be relieved of his duties for the race, and Riddle's further requirement that the match be started by flag rather than with the usual starting gate, which he (or his horse) disliked: the substitute starter would drop a flag and ring a bell as the horses walked up to the starting line. Howard, a rather less fussy owner, went along with his opponent's stipulations. Vanderbilt undertook that the track would put up $10,000 and each owner

$5000, that stake to be forfeited in the case of withdrawal.

Of the two, Seabiscuit had endured the tougher campaign before 1 November, carrying big weights heroically – and sometimes successfully – in handicaps and winning a match against the Argentine-bred horse Ligaroti (owned by the Binglin Stock Farm, the stable name of Bing Crosby and Lin Howard, son of Seabiscuit's owner). Two weeks before the Pimlico Special he had run second to the three-year-old filly Jacola (conceding her twenty-four pounds) in the Laurel Stakes over one mile. War Admiral had won an allowance race in Florida on 19 February and two handicaps before defeat in the Massachusetts Handicap; he then notched up five victories off the reel, culminating in a facile success in the Jockey Club Gold Cup over two miles at Belmont Park. He would be reverting to a distance six and a half furlongs shorter than that in taking on Seabiscuit at Pimlico.

A further contrast between the two lay in their style of running. Seabiscuit tended to save his energies for a burst of power up the home stretch, while War Admiral would blaze off in front and run his opponents into the ground in the first three furlongs. How could Seabiscuit counter that?

By the time the entrance gates were opened long lines had formed, and 40,000 people were crammed into the stands as the time for the Special, the seventh race on the programme, approached. As War Admiral was led past the spectators on the way to the paddock behind the new clubhouse he drew applause: head high and trotting with a measured step, he was the picture of readiness. A few minutes later Seabiscuit appeared. Though almost as small as his rival at 15 hands $2^1/_2$ inches, he was heavier of frame and seemed less keyed up. His connections were less keyed up as well, for he would be ridden by the imperturbable George 'Ice Man' Woolf, and the chief concern of his trainer 'Silent' Tom Smith, according to one account of the occasion, 'seemed to be finding a place to spit without hitting a spectator'. The jockeys were thrown up into their saddles – Woolf on Seabiscuit, Charley Kurtsinger on War Admiral – and the hubbub of the crowd died into a tense silence.

Despite reverting to nine and a half furlongs after running over two miles, War Admiral seemed to have watertight credentials, and the betting made him look a certainty: 4–1 on to beat Seabiscuit at 11–5.

War Admiral had drawn the inside berth – ideal for his trail-blazing front-running from the fall of the flag. As starter George Cassidy called them in the Triple Crown winner lunged forwards, and Cassidy sent them back. Then Seabiscuit tried to anticipate the start, and they were sent back again. By the third time of asking a complete hush had fallen over Pimlico, and as Cassidy finally got them away at this attempt the clang of his bell could be clearly heard. An instant later a bedlam of confusion broke out, for the unanticipated had happened: Seabiscuit, the horse who saved his energies for the final stretch, had broken in front, and War Admiral was soon a length behind. Woolf had thwacked Seabiscuit with the whip as soon as the flag fell and kept working away at him

until he had moved over to take the rail, and as they came down the home stretch for the first time War Admiral, quite unable to make his own running, was two lengths adrift. By the clubhouse turn he had settled in behind, nose to tail, and as they straightened out in the back stretch Kurtsinger gave him a dose of the whip, bringing him level with his rival by the five-furlong pole. A great cheer broke out as War Admiral came alongside, but as the two hammered down the far side of the track Seabiscuit was still a nose in front. For all of three furious furlongs they remained head to head, eyeball to eyeball, and as they started round the home turn the whips were out in earnest – Woolf's to keep Seabiscuit up to his task, Kurtsinger's desperately trying to force War Admiral to the front. Down the home stretch Seabiscuit still held a narrow advantage, but just when it seemed that War Admiral would come through to assert his superiority the unthinkable happened: Seabiscuit started to go away. A neck, half a length, and then daylight appeared between the two: Seabiscuit had led throughout, and still had the power for his accustomed surge to the line! War Admiral's spirit broke, and at the wire Seabiscuit was four lengths to the good. He had recorded a track record time of 1 minute 56.6 seconds, and he had slaughtered his famous rival in a manner which few could have foreseen. Not that such matters seemed to bother the horse, who casually nibbled chrysanthemums from the wreath in the winner's circle.

An injury early in the 1939 season kept Seabiscuit off the course until the following year, when he won the San Antonio Handicap and the Santa Anita Handicap and was then retired, at the age of seven, the world's leading money-earner at $437,730. War Admiral won his first race of 1939 before contracting laryngitis. A subsequent ankle injury forced his retirement from a brilliant career in which he had won twenty-one of his twenty-five races.

The American journalist Grantland Rice summed up the moment of truth for War Admiral: 'He had never met a horse who could look him in the eye down the stretch and say to him in horse language, "Now let's start travelling, kid. How do you feel? I feel great. This is down my alley".'

## Pimlico Special

Pimlico
1 mile 1$^1/_2$ furlongs
1 November 1938

| | | |
|---|---|---|
| 1 Seabiscuit | G. Woolf | 11–5 |
| 2 War Admiral | C. Kurtsinger | 1–4 fav. |

2 ran

Winner owned by C. S. Howard, trained by T. Smith

*Distance*: 4 lengths

# NASHWAN AND CACOETHES

*King George VI and Queen Elizabeth Diamond Stakes*
*Ascot, 22 July 1989*

*Nashwan (left) and Cacoethes pull clear of Top Class (obscured by Nashwan), Carroll House (yellow cap) and Sheriff's Star (grey with sheepskin noseband).*

**♦ He had a terrific stride and could turn it on ♦**

How good a racehorse was Nashwan? The International Classification for three-year-olds, drawn up by the official handicappers, rated both Old Vic and Zilzal his superiors. But there is no doubt that for a few brief weeks during the scorching summer of 1989 it was Nashwan who lit up the European Flat racing scene, and the memory of this tall chestnut with the voracious, ground-devouring stride will not fade quickly.

Owned by Sheikh Hamdan Al-Maktoum, trained at West Ilsley by Major Dick Hern and ridden in all his races by Willie Carson,

Nashwan had what is now a typical two-year-old campaign for a horse with pretensions to the Classics: he took a maiden race at Newbury in August before winning at Ascot in October. Behind him in third place at Ascot, beaten four and a half lengths, was a horse named Cacoethes; they would meet twice more. Although Nashwan's two-year-old form had been encouraging it had not been of the order to suggest that he was anything remarkable; but the Classic picture was transformed when news filtered out of West Ilsley that he had been working spectacularly well in his preparation for the Two

Thousand Guineas, and in the week before the race he became the focus of all market attention. Backed down to 3–1 favourite on the day, he justified the support by charging up the Newmarket hill to defeat Exbourne, and was then aimed at the Ever Ready Derby. Meanwhile Cacoethes, who had run only the once as a juvenile, came into the Derby picture with easy wins at Brighton and Lingfield, and for a time shortly before the Epsom Classic vied with Nashwan for favouritism. But as the going softened, support for Major Hern's runner did the opposite, and on the day Cacoethes started second favourite, with Nashwan heavily backed at 5–4. Storming home five lengths clear of 500–1 outsider Terimon, with Cacoethes two lengths further back in third, Nashwan became the first horse since Nijinsky in 1970 to win both the Derby and the Guineas. The manner of his victory – he bounded home with tremendous zest, his giant stride eating up the ground in the final furlong – suggested that he could be one of the great horses of modern times, and his performance in his next race, the Coral-Eclipse Stakes at Sandown Park, did nothing to alter that view. Again it was the giant stride which caught the eye and the imagination.

No horse had ever won the Two Thousand Guineas, the Derby, the Eclipse and the King George VI and Queen Elizabeth Stakes in the same season, but although the Ascot race came only two weeks after the Eclipse it was generally felt that it would be a formality for the Derby winner. The one horse whose presence would have made the 1989 King George the true middle-distance championship of Europe was Old Vic, who had won the Prix du Jockey-Club Lancia and the Budweiser Irish Derby in scintillating fashion, but he was injured, and had to miss the race, leaving just six opponents to take on Nashwan. The only other three-year-old was Cacoethes, ridden as usual by Greville Starkey: since the Derby he had won the King Edward VII Stakes at Royal Ascot but seemed to have little chance of reversing Epsom form with Nashwan. Of the four-year-olds, Sheriff's Star had won the Hanson Coronation Cup at Epsom and the Grand Prix de Saint-Cloud and Carroll House the Princess of Wales's Stakes at Newmarket, while Top

Class had run second in the Hardwicke Stakes at Royal Ascot and the Italian challenger Tisserand had won the Derby Italiano in 1988. The field was completed by the five-year-old Polemos, there to ensure a good pace for Nashwan.

Cacoethes was a size smaller than his rival but extremely well-muscled and looked fit to run for his life. Nashwan was long, rangy, deep-girthed and tall, but even halfway through his three-year-old season he looked immature and unfurnished. He started at 9–2 on, with Cacoethes at 6–1 and Sheriff's Star at 10–1 the only remotely possible alternatives.

Polemos sent a fairly steady pace in the early stages, and after a mile gave way as Top Class shot into the lead. As the runners swung into the short Ascot straight it seemed for a moment as if the enterprising tactics of Michael Roberts on Top Class might bring a shock result, for he had gone several lengths clear. Nashwan was not a horse who could accelerate instantly, and it took Willie Carson a few moments to get him into top gear. Once at full speed, however, he got to Top Class halfway up the straight – receiving a hefty bump in the process – and inside the final quarter of a mile had taken the lead. But just as he seemed about to pull away for another decisive victory Cacoethes – who had been pocketed on the rails coming round the home turn but had accelerated smartly on reaching the straight – came at him, and for a furlong and a half they slogged it out, Nashwan on the far side, Cacoethes on the stands side, Nashwan clawing away with his huge stride, the leaner Cacoethes straining every sinew to stay with him. For a moment it looked as though Starkey had got Cacoethes in front – perhaps by a neck – but then Nashwan dug deep for reserves of courage and guts which he had never before been called upon to muster, and as they hurtled towards the winning post he regained the upper hand. Cacoethes was not stopping, but Nashwan was just the stronger, and he held on by a neck. Top Class was seven lengths back in third.

The King George had shown that Nashwan had grit and strength when they were needed, for Cacoethes had pushed him to the limit. But anti-climax was to follow.

**King George VI and Queen Elizabeth Diamond Stakes**

Ascot
1½ miles
22 July 1989

| 1 Nashwan | W. Carson | 2–9 fav. |
| 2 Cacoethes | G. Starkey | 6–1 |
| 3 Top Class | M. Roberts | 50–1 |

*Also ran:* Sheriff's Star (4th), Carroll House, Polemos, Tisserand

7 ran

Winner owned by H. Al-Maktoum, trained by W. R. Hern

*Distances:* neck, 7 lengths

*At the post Nashwan holds on.*

Cacoethes was sensationally defeated at 5–2 on by his stable companion Ile De Chypre in the Juddmonte International Stakes at York the following month and ended the season by running a dismal sixteenth of nineteen behind Carroll House (eleven lengths behind him in the King George) in the Prix de l'Arc de Triomphe. It was widely hoped that Nashwan would go for the Triple Crown by running in the St Leger, but instead he went to Longchamp for the Prix Niel as his warm-up race for the Arc and suffered the first defeat of his life, running a crushingly disappointing third to Golden Pheasant. Plans to return to Longchamp for the Arc were promptly dropped, but it was intended to finish his racing career in the Champion Stakes at Newmarket. Sadly he developed a temperature during the week before the race and was retired. His career had consisted of seven races.

If we will never know just how good Nashwan could have been, we at least have the opinion of Willie Carson, the man most likely to know: 'A great horse to ride, he had a terrific stride and could turn it on.'

# DUNFERMLINE AND ALLEGED

*St Leger Stakes*
*Doncaster, 10 September 1977*

❛ *I was right up his gear-box, and Lester knew I was there* ❜

*Shortly after the start, Dunfermline (black cap) is tucked in behind Lucky Sovereign (no. 7), with Lester Piggott's bottom confidently pitched on Alleged between them.*

The St Leger, the oldest Classic, is not a race for the faint-hearted. It comes towards the end of the season, when many of the runners may be feeling the effects of earlier efforts, it is run over a distance of further than one and three quarter miles, and it culminates in an extended slog up the wide Doncaster straight, nearly five furlongs long. If it has produced many famous races, none was more exciting or yielded a result so widely welcomed as that of 1977, the year of Dunfermline and Alleged.

Owned and bred by Queen Elizabeth II, the three-year-old filly Dunfermline had already sent the racing world into raptures once in 1977 when winning the Oaks. For this was the year of the Queen's Silver Jubi-

lee, and Dunfermline's hard-won victory at Epsom came only three days before the procession through London to St Paul's Cathedral which formed the central event of the Jubilee celebrations. A filly whose strong suit was stamina, she had then finished a disappointing third in a slowly run Yorkshire Oaks before being aimed by trainer Dick Hern at the St Leger, where she would be suited by a distance more than a quarter of a mile longer than her previous runs and would be sure to get the strong gallop necessary to bring out her best.

What would certainly test her to the full was the presence in the field of Alleged. Trained by the Irish genius Vincent O'Brien, this three-year-old looked to be a real superstar in the making, and was unbeaten in four

*Dunfermline battles past Alleged.*

races in 1977 after winning on his only outing as a two-year-old. This season he had won a small race at Leopardstown before taking the Royal Whip Stakes and the Gallinule Stakes – both Pattern races – at The Curragh. He had then turned in a sensational performance in the Great Voltigeur Stakes at York's August Meeting, coming clean away from a good field (which included Hot Grove, who had all but beaten Alleged's distinguished stable-companion The Minstrel in a throbbing finish to the Derby). Ridden in the St Leger by Lester Piggott, he was unsurprisingly quoted at the very short price of 7–4 on, the hottest favourite for the race since Nijinsky (7–2 on) in 1970.

Dunfermline, partnered by Willie Carson, started at 10–1 at Doncaster, for Alleged appeared to be unbeatable and her own performance at York had suggested that as Oaks winners go she was probably no better than average. Sadly, affairs of state demanded the Queen's presence elsewhere (at Balmoral, to welcome Prime Minister James Callaghan), just as the Jubilee celebrations had prevented her witnessing her filly's victory in the Oaks.

Thirteen horses went to post, including three challengers from France and Olwyn, a filly who had won the Irish Oaks after being well beaten behind Dunfermline at Epsom. The colts Lucky Sovereign and Classic Example had both been walloped by Alleged at York and had no real chance of turning the tables. Whichever way you approached it, the 1977 St Leger looked like a benefit for Alleged, just the thing to put him right for the Prix de l'Arc de Triomphe in Paris the following month.

It didn't quite work out like that. In the early stages the Queen's other runner Gregarious, taking part to ensure a sound gallop for the principal Royal entry and not wholly without the chance of a place in his own right, made the running with Piggott sitting second on Alleged and Dunfermline about fifth, all in a closely bunched field. Coming towards the straight Willie Carson, alert to the fact that Piggott could use Alleged's speed to slip his field at any time, moved Dunfermline up into third, and once in line for home Alleged did indeed set sail, going easily past Gregarious. Dunfermline followed him through and sat in behind. 'I was right up his gear-box, and Lester knew I was there', said Willie Carson later, and when Piggott saw Carson in his slipstream he kicked on. With two furlongs to go both horses were at full pelt and it seemed as though Alleged was galloping strongly enough to withstand the gallant challenge of the Queen's filly, but she just would not be shaken off. Carson brought her out to make her run on the stands side and she started to overhaul her rival. Exchanging the nonchalant confidence of a few seconds before for the full force which formed the other side of his remarkable riding character, Piggott got to work with a vengeance, but it was Carson, pumping away in his extraordinarily energetic fashion, who took a slight lead in the final furlong. Alleged, desperately tired, came away from the rails and hung into Piggott's whip, while Dunfermline, now under the strongest pressure from her jockey, hung away from the whip towards the colt. Moments later Dunfermline had gone clear, Carson put down his whip and rode her to the finish with hands and heels, and Piggott accepted defeat.

The bare statistic that Dunfermline won by a length and a half does no justice to the closeness and excitement of the race, for the two had drawn ten lengths clear of third-placed Classic Example and produced a thrilling contest. Nor was the excitement over yet, for they had come very close together in the final desperate stages, and it was no surprise that a Stewards' Enquiry was announced. The head-on film of the race showed clearly that the two horses had not touched, but it was only after a tense twenty minutes of deliberation that the result was allowed to stand.

Three weeks later Dunfermline and Alleged met again in the Prix de l'Arc de Triomphe over a mile and a half at Longchamp. To no one's great surprise, Alleged reversed the Doncaster form; but Dunfermline ran a fine race to finish a close-up fourth. The following season Alleged won the Arc again while Dunfermline disappointed bitterly, failing to win at three attempts. But on her day she was possibly the most brilliant horse the Queen has ever owned.

# NORTHERN DANCER AND HILL RISE

*Kentucky Derby*
*Churchill Downs, 2 May 1964*

**Kentucky Derby**

Churchill Downs
1¼ miles
2 May 1964

| | | |
|---|---|---|
| 1 Northern Dancer | W. Hartack | 34–10 |
| 2 Hill Rise | W. Shoemaker | 14–10 fav. |
| 3 The Scoundrel | M. Ycaza | 6–1 |

*Also ran:* Roman Brother (4th), Quadrangle, Mr Brick, Mr Moonlight, Dandy K, Ishkoodah, Wil Rad, Extra Swell, Royal Shuck

12 ran

Winner owned by Windfields Farm, trained by H. A. Luro

*Distances:* neck, 3¼ lengths

▌ *He's all blood and guts and he tries hard* ▌

Sire of Nijinsky, Lyphard, Nureyev, El Gran Senor, Secreto, The Minstrel, Shareef Dancer, Sadler's Wells and so many other brilliant horses, Northern Dancer has exerted such a profound influence on the modern bloodstock industry that his career as a stallion has tended to overshadow his own achievements on the racecourse. Yet this little horse – just 15.2 hands high – was the greatest performer in the history of Canadian racing, and only failed to win the US Triple Crown through his stamina giving out in the Belmont Stakes.

Northern Dancer was born on 27 May 1961, a son of Nearctic, himself a son of the great Italian horse Nearco. At the yearling sales he failed to reach his reserve of $25,000 and was returned to his breeder E. P. Taylor, who put him into training with Horatio Luro. At first he reacted adversely to the training routine, doing everything in his power to dislodge his rider and generally proving a disruptive influence, but his excesses of temper began to seem forgivable when he won five of his seven two-year-old races in Canada. He then travelled south to take on the crack American two-year-old Bupers at Aqueduct, and beat him eight lengths. One more victory as a two-year-old, and with a score of seven wins out of nine runs the Triple Crown races the following year started to beckon.

His first race as a three-year-old was in Florida, where he was beaten by Chieftain. His jockey on that occasion, Bob Ussery, had used his whip on the little colt against the trainer's instructions, and he was replaced by Bill Shoemaker in the Flamingo Stakes and the Florida Derby. Northern Dancer won both. Shoemaker was then expected to partner the colt in the Kentucky Derby, but opted instead for the big Californian horse Hill Rise, winner of the Santa Anita Derby, and the ride on Northern Dancer went to Bill Hartack. A Pennsylvania coal miner's son noted for his irascibility and bluntness ('The madder I get, the better I ride'), Hartack had already won the Derby three times so knew exactly what was required, and his first ride on Northern Dancer was a confidence-boosting win in the Blue Grass Stakes at Keeneland. But if his relationship with his fellow jockeys was frosty, with the press it was Arc-

tic: the day before the Derby he had passed up a ride at Churchill Downs in order to go into the press box to argue with the racing journalists – 'in a manner not always in good taste and that goes for both sides', reported the *Washington Post*. (Twenty-six years later the West Indies cricket captain Viv Richards would similarly take time off from competing in order to berate the press. In neither case did the distraction prove detrimental to winning chances.)

As the largest Kentucky Derby crowd on record stood in time-honoured fashion to intone *My Old Kentucky Home*, it was Shoemaker and Hill Rise who were attracting the support at the betting windows, and at the off the Californian horse was a hot favourite. Northern Dancer was second favourite, paying 34–10; of the ten others, only The Scoundrel and Quadrangle were paying less than 10–1.

Northern Dancer was drawn in the middle of the field and broke well as Royal Shuck took an early lead and then gave way to Mr Brick, who led for the first mile before capitulating quickly when Northern Dancer, who had been running in sixth position on the inside rail, moved up rapidly to challenge. Coming round the final turn The Scoundrel came up into second, forcing Northern Dancer to move out in order to take the lead. Hartack was hard at it with the whip as the runners careered into the home stretch and his colt was responding gamely, but now Hill Rise, who had suffered interference down the back stretch, was being brought round wide by Shoemaker. Northern Dancer had the rails and had gone into a two-length lead, but Hill Rise was rallying and gaining ground with every stride, and the two left their rivals toiling. Northern Dancer's decisive spurt in the back stretch had surprised Shoemaker and left Hill Rise flat-footed, and now it was a case of whether the little horse could hold on as his bigger rival launched his attack. All the way up the straight Hill Rise was coming closer, but Northern Dancer was a tough customer, and with the rails to help him he maintained his advantage. Shoemaker forced Hill Rise to Northern Dancer's quarters, then to his girth, but the wire was rapidly approaching and the Canadian horse did not falter. Hartack was riding a powerhouse finish and thwacking Northern Dancer regularly down his left side, and the colt kept up the gallop with great courage to win a stirring race by a neck. The Scoundrel kept on to finish third, over three lengths behind Hill Rise.

The time for the race – two minutes dead – set a new track record, and Northern Dancer had done it twenty-five days short of his true third birthday.

Hartack's attitude towards the press did not mellow in the afterglow of victory. He kept the racing journalists waiting for over an hour as he signed autographs outside the jockeys' room, and when eventually he went in to face the journalists he would not pronounce upon the race until certain writers of whom he did not approve – 'There are some guys I won't talk to' – left the room. Had these three been pressing their ears to the keyhole they would have heard Hartack pay tribute to Northern Dancer: 'I put him to a hard drive, hitting him hard all the way … He's a good little horse. He's all blood and guts and he tries hard.'

In the second leg of the Triple Crown, the Preakness at Pimlico, Northern Dancer and Hill Rise met again. Plenty of people felt that Hill Rise had been unlucky in the Derby, and

again he was sent off the odds-on favourite. Hill Rise was upsides Northern Dancer coming round the final turn but the Canadian colt asserted his superiority by pulling away to win by two and a quarter lengths as Hill Rise just lost second place to The Scoundrel. Now the Triple Crown looked there for the taking, but the twelve furlongs of the Belmont Stakes proved too far for Northern Dancer, and he was beaten into third place behind Quadrangle and Roman Brother.

Northern Dancer then returned to Canada, where he won the Queen's Plate by seven and a half lengths and was afforded a rousing reception by his home crowd. Soon after that he injured a tendon at exercise and retired, having won fourteen of his eighteen starts.

He commenced his stud career in Canada before transferring to his breeder's Windfields Farm in Maryland, where he was syndicated for $2,400,000: this handsome sum began to look measly as he became the most influential sire in the world. By the mid-1980s his reputation was such that a nomination to him, on the rare occasions when one came on to the market, was reported to be worth $800,000. He finally retired from stud duties in 1987.

*Northern Dancer holds off Hill Rise.*

# MTOTO AND REFERENCE POINT

*Eclipse Stakes*
*Sandown Park, 4 July 1987*

❛ *Then I saw we'd got him* ❜

*Mtoto (near side) stretches clear of Reference Point.*

The 1987 Coral-Eclipse Stakes was one of those races which had greatness thrust upon it. For while it had seemed in prospect to be probably at the mercy of that year's Derby winner, the relentless front-runner Reference Point, in the event it produced a memorable finish.

The first big race to bring middle-distance Classic three-year-olds up against the best of the older generations, the Eclipse Stakes had produced many famous races, including the 1903 clash of Ard Patrick, Sceptre and Rock Sand (described on pages 18–19), the dead-heat in 1910 between the Two Thousand Guineas winner Neil Gow and the Derby winner Lemberg, and the 1968 running when the previous year's Derby winner Royal Palace beat French challenger Taj Dewan by a short head, with that year's Derby hero Sir Ivor three quarters of a length back in third (pages 52–3). In the mid-1980s the quality of Eclipse fields was extremely high, with Sadler's Wells winning

in 1984, Pebbles in 1985 becoming the first filly ever to win the race when beating subsequent Arc winner Rainbow Quest, and Dancing Brave making up for his unfortunate Derby defeat by slamming Triptych and Teleprompter.

The field for 1987 was well up to standard. Louis Freedman's Reference Point, trained at Newmarket by Henry Cecil and ridden by Steve Cauthen, was clearly the best three-year-old of his generation. After winning the William Hill Futurity as a two-year-old he had opened his next season's campaign with victory in the Mecca-Dante Stakes at York, where the rather workmanlike nature of his performance was put down to a preparation interrupted by a sinus complaint; in the Ever Ready Derby at Epsom he led almost from the start and stayed on gamely to beat Most Welcome by a length and a half. He was the first Derby winner to run in the Eclipse since his sire Mill Reef in 1971.

Reference Point was expected to win: but

*Photographed from a more hazardous angle, Mtoto (right) and Reference Point go for the line.*

it would be no formality, for among his seven opponents were some high-class performers. From France came Triptych, now a five-year-old but still as able and as tough as ever; her two races before coming to Sandown Park had been two more Group One wins – the Prix Ganay at Longchamp and the Hanson Trust Coronation Cup at Epsom. Bellotto had been beaten a neck by Don't Forget Me in the Two Thousand Guineas and then had run a close third to Reference Point in the Derby, and Milligram had won the Coronation Stakes at Royal Ascot.

And then there was Mtoto. Trained by Alec Stewart and very lightly raced as a two-year-old, he bypassed the Classics at three but ran well enough in the best company to suggest that as a late-maturing colt he would really come into his own at four. And so it proved. In his 1987 reappearance, the Brigadier Gerard Stakes at Sandown Park, he started at 16–1 but showed a devastating turn of foot to upset the odds laid on Allez Milord. At Royal Ascot the same acceleration whisked him home in the Prince of Wales's Stakes.

This was excellent form, but it was not of a calibre to suggest that Mtoto could beat the Derby winner, and for the Eclipse he started at 6–1, joint third favourite with Bellotto behind Reference Point (evens favourite) and Triptych (4–1). Steve Cauthen was aboard Reference Point, with Tony Cruz on Triptych and Michael Roberts on Mtoto.

The race was run on a baking hot and sunny Saturday, and the scorching weather was matched by the early pace as Cauthen on Reference Point sought to use the front-running tactics which had worked so triumphantly in the Derby. This race, two furlongs shorter than the Classic, laid less emphasis on stamina, and Reference Point needed to stretch his rivals from the start. As he left the stalls Reference Point's saddle slipped, and it took Cauthen the best part of a furlong to wrench it back into place. But this hardly proved any inconvenience, and soon Reference Point was setting such a blistering gallop that Media Starguest, whose role in the race was to set a strong pace for Triptych, could never get to the front. Reference Point hammering along the far side at Sandown Park on a blazing afternoon – mane

unplaited like most of Henry Cecil's runners – made a glorious sight, and even before the field had started to make the turn out of the back straight, with some six furlongs to go, half of his rivals were already struggling. The sweeping turn towards the stands at Sandown ensures that there is no appreciable let-up in the pace, and Reference Point, taking full advantage of one of the most galloping courses in the country, levelled up for home and the haul up the hill two lengths in front, with every appearance of staying there all the way to the line. But by the two-furlong marker Mtoto had detached himself from the following group and was in full pursuit of his younger rival (to whom he was conceding, under weight-for-age terms, thirteen pounds). An unforgettable neck-and-neck duel ensued, both horses stretched out to the limit, and both jockeys riding forcefully but in complete sympathy with the efforts of their mounts. At the furlong pole it looked as though Reference Point would hang on, but, according to Roberts, 'then I saw we'd got him.' The jockey conjured a final effort out of Mtoto and he inched ahead. Just before the line Reference Point came again but his final fling was unavailing, and at the post Mtoto had three quarters of a length to spare. Triptych, who had to be switched to deliver her challenge, ran on to be third, a length and half behind the runner-up.

It had been a desperate struggle, but unlike many such races it did not seem to leave a lasting mark on the contestants, for both horses went on to enhance their reputations. Reference Point won the King George VI and Queen Elizabeth Diamond Stakes at Ascot later in July and the Great Voltigeur Stakes at York *en route* to the St Leger, where he became the first Derby winner since Nijinsky in 1970 to win the final Classic; an injured foot explained his odds-on failure in the Prix de l'Arc de Triomphe. Mtoto, although fourth in that Arc and then a disappointment in the Champion Stakes, had a brilliant campaign the following season, winning the Eclipse again (by a neck from Shady Heights) and the King George (from Unfuwain), before a narrow defeat by Tony Bin in the Arc.

# JUPITER ISLAND AND ALLEZ MILORD

*Japan Cup*
*Tokyo, 23 November 1986*

**Japan Cup**

Tokyo
1½ miles
23 November 1986

| | | |
|---|---|---|
| 1 Jupiter Island | P. Eddery | 139–10 |
| 2 Allez Milord | G. Starkey | 87–10 |
| 3 Miho Shinzan | M. Shibata | 13–2 |

*Also ran:* Rugby Ball (4th), Waverley Star, Sakura Yutaka, Jusaburo, Kushiro King, Carotene, Gallop Dyna, Triptych, Flying Pidgeon, Tommy Way, Suda Hawk

14 ran

Winner owned by Lord Tavistock, trained by C. Brittain

*Distances:* head, 1¼ lengths

❧ *Brittain sometimes rivals Don Quixote in tilting at windmills* ❧

In 1981 Japanese racing moved on to the international stage with the inaugural running of the Japan Cup, a twelve-furlong Flat race run at Tokyo over the oval turf course. Now a major event in the racing calendar and an important element of the Japanese racing and breeding industry's drive to establish itself in world racing, the Japan Cup is an invitation race designed to bring to the Orient the best horses from the main arenas of top-class sport in both the northern and the southern hemispheres. By the time of the 1986 running it had fulfilled this purpose to great effect, with three of the first five winners coming from overseas – Mairzy Doates and Half Iced from the USA, Stanerra from Ireland – and the other two runnings going to the home-trained Katsuragi Ace and Symboli Rudolph.

The field for the 1986 race was typical. The fourteen runners comprised seven local horses and seven from overseas, with the United States, New Zealand and Canada providing runners in addition to the globe-trotting Triptych from France and three challengers from Britain: Jupiter Island, Allez Milord and Tommy Way. Although none of these was in the very top bracket, each had form which justified his presence in the line-up for the race. Tommy Way was a seasoned traveller, having won the Derby Italiano Lancia at Rome and the Gran Premio di Milano as well as a Group Two race at Hamburg. Allez Milord was one of the better three-year-olds in Britain, winner of the Schroder Predominate Stakes and the Gordon Stakes, both at Goodwood, and he too had clocked up plenty of air-miles, winning the Puma Europa Preis at Cologne. For seven-year-old Jupiter Island the Japan Cup was only his third race of the season but he had already been on his travels back in April, running a good third in the San Juan Capistrano handicap at Santa Anita, California, despite suffering from a foot complaint which caused his absence from the track for the next six months. He returned to action to win the St Simon Stakes at Newbury in late October, and was then dispatched east for two weeks' acclimatization before the big day. The oldest horse in the race, Jupiter Island was tough and durable but was hardly in the same league as the likes of Triptych,

who had won the Champion Stakes at Newmarket since running a close third to Dancing Brave in the Arc (see pages 104–6); after that, however, she had run unplaced on dirt in the Breeders' Cup Classic, and it seemed that the strain of a long season in which she had undertaken a great deal of travel might be beginning to affect her. Strictly on form Jupiter Island looked to be a trifle out of his depth, but Clive Brittain, who trained the horse for owner Lord Tavistock, had never been one not to have a go; 'Brittain sometimes rivals Don Quixote in tilting at windmills,' according to the Timeform organization, but again he was to be rewarded.

The betting at the off had the local horse Sakura Yutaka favourite at 31–10, with the New Zealand challenger Waverley Star at 7–2 and Triptych 6–1. Of the three British raiders, Allez Milord was most fancied at 87–10, with Jupiter Island at 139–10 and Tommy Way an outsider at 272–10. The going was firm, and the runners went at a tremendous rate in the early stages; and at the turn for home it was Greville Starkey on Allez Milord who took over the lead and set off for the line, going so strongly that it seemed he could not be caught. Pat Eddery on Jupiter Island, though, had other ideas and set off in pursuit: as soon as Jupiter Island had got to Allez Milord a furious battle was engaged, and the two ran through the last two hundred yards locked together. At one point it looked as if Allez Milord's class would assert itself, but Jupiter Island had long had a reputation as a horse who could call on extraordinary reserves of courage and they did not desert him now. Neck thrust out and responding to Eddery's every urging, he kept doggedly to his task, and forced himself a head in front of his rival at the line. The best of the Japanese horses was Miho Shinzan, one and a quarter lengths behind Allez Milord in third. It had been a desperate finish, and the two principals had appeared to come into contact with each other, but a Stewards' Enquiry did not alter the placings. The time of the race was an extraordinarily fast 2 minutes 25 seconds.

Jupiter Island had more than doubled his career earnings with this hard-earned success and was retired to stud. Allez Milord did

*Jupiter Island (near side) beats Allez Milord, with Miho Shinzan third.*

not run again that season but in 1987 matured into a fine four-year-old, waltzing home in the Gordon Richards Stakes at Sandown Park and later in the season moving to the USA, where he won the Oak Tree Invitational Stakes in his first run for his new stable. Triptych, who finished a tired eleventh, was fourth in the race the following year.

# ROYAL PALACE, TAJ DEWAN AND SIR IVOR
### Eclipse Stakes
### Sandown Park, 6 July 1968

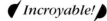
*Incroyable!*

In 1968 the Eclipse Stakes brought into opposition two winners of the Epsom Derby for the first time in the race since Ard Patrick and Rock Sand had clashed in 1903 (see pages 18–19), and in setting against one another top horses from England, Ireland and France it produced a contest of very similar stature.

Royal Palace had won the Two Thousand Guineas and the Derby in 1967 but a leg injury ruined his chance of a bid for the Triple Crown and his season ended in anticlimax with a third behind Reform and Taj Dewan (whom he had beaten a short head after a memorable tussle in the Guineas) in the Champion Stakes at Newmarket. The decision by owner Jim Joel and trainer Noel Murless to keep him in training as a four-year-old was soon vindicated with victories in the Coronation Stakes at Sandown Park, the Coronation Cup at Epsom and the Prince of Wales's Stakes at Royal Ascot, but the Eclipse would be his sternest test to date.

And it could hardly be sterner, for lining up against him was the brilliant Sir Ivor, trained by Vincent O'Brien and ridden by Lester Piggott. Like Royal Palace, Sir Ivor had won the Two Thousand Guineas and the Derby (in which he showed a remarkable turn of foot to beat Connaught by one and a half lengths), but had then been beaten at 3–1 on in the Irish Derby by Ribero, ridden by Piggott as the ride on Sir Ivor in Ireland went to Liam Ward. So Sir Ivor came to Sandown Park just a week after defeat at The Curragh looking to redeem a slightly tarnished reputation, but it was widely felt that the ten furlongs of the Eclipse was his ideal trip, and he was made favourite to resume his winning ways.

Third in the betting was Royal Palace's old rival Taj Dewan, ridden by Yves Saint-Martin. The French-trained colt had won the important Prix Ganay at Longchamp in April and had clearly trained on into one of the best four-year-olds in France; nevertheless, although he had run Royal Palace so close in the 1967 Two Thousand Guineas he started 7–2 third favourite for the Eclipse, with Royal Palace 9–4 and Sir Ivor the hot favourite at 5–4 on. The other two runners – Frankincense, who had won the Lincoln Handicap under top weight, and another

French challenger Franc Castel – were 50–1 outsiders.

The going was fast, the crowd huge, and as the runners circled at the start the screws of expectant tension were wound tight. This was the essence of what the Eclipse Stakes had been designed to achieve on its foundation more than eighty years ago – the best middle-distance horses of different generations and from different countries meeting on weight-for-age terms on one of the fairest racecourses in Europe.

Sandy Barclay on Royal Palace was content to lie in third place in the early stages of the race, and as Franc Castel led at a brisk pace round the long right-handed sweep into the straight none of the riders of the three principals was ready to make a move. Levelled up for home, and with four and a half furlongs of the Sandown hill ahead to expose any weaknesses, Franc Castel was still at the head of affairs – but clearly on sufferance, for behind him Taj Dewan, Royal Palace and Sir Ivor were all poised. It was Saint-Martin on Taj Dewan who made the first move, and as Franc Castel weakened with about half a mile to run Taj Dewan found himself in the lead and going for home at full pelt. For a furlong or so it seemed as if Saint-Martin's decision not to hang about once the pacemaker had weakened would pay off, for with over a furlong to go Piggott was three lengths adrift and hard at work on Sir Ivor as he tried to make his challenge up the centre of the course, and although Barclay had galvanized Royal Palace into action Taj Dewan had the rails berth and was not weakening. With a furlong to go Sir Ivor was clearly beaten and it looked as though Taj Dewan would hold on, but amid delirious encouragement from the stands Royal Palace kept closing the gap inch by inch. Both jockeys were riding supremely rhythmical finishes and both horses were giving everything, and they flashed past the winning post seemingly inseparable. Sir Ivor had rallied in the final furlong and at the line was less than a length behind the leading pair in third place.

It had been a titanic race, and a dead heat would have been a fair result. Yves Saint-Martin and Taj Dewan's trainer Robert Corme were convinced that they had won,

**Eclipse Stakes**

Sandown Park
1¼ miles
6 July 1968

| | | |
|---|---|---|
| 1 Royal Palace | A. Barclay | 9–4 |
| 2 Taj Dewan | Y. Saint-Martin | 7–2 |
| 3 Sir Ivor | L. Piggott | 4–5 fav. |

*Also ran:* Frankincense (4th), Franc Castel

5 ran

Winner owned by H. J. Joel, trained by N. Murless

*Distances:* short head, ¾ length

*Royal Palace (no. 4) gets up to pip Taj Dewan (near side) and Sir Ivor.*

and this view was widely shared as the result of the photograph was awaited: bookmakers were betting as short as 8–1 on the French horse getting the race. But the angle at Sandown Park is notoriously difficult to read in a very close finish, and few finishes there have ever been as close as this. The photo finish revealed that Royal Palace had got up, to win by a short head – a couple of inches. Some of the French contingent would not even believe the evidence of the photograph, though Corme and Saint-Martin accepted the result with reactions of '*incroyable*!' and '*impossible*!' respectively.

Three weeks later Royal Palace won the King George VI and Queen Elizabeth Stakes at Ascot. but he finished very lame and did not race again. He was retired to stud, where he numbered the triple Champion Hurdle winner See You Then among his offspring. Taj Dewan likewise ran just once more, finishing a disappointing fifth to Sir Ivor in the Champion Stakes. Before the Champion victory Sir Ivor had been beaten in his preparation race for the Prix de l'Arc de Triomphe and had run second to the great Vaguely Noble in the Arc itself; he then ended his career in triumphant style with his controversial win the Washington International (see pages 139–40).

# FERDINAND AND ALYSHEBA

*Breeders' Cup Classic*
*Hollywood Park, 21 November 1987*

◀ *Ferdinand just kept digging in* ▶

In 1979 Affirmed and Spectacular Bid clashed in the Jockey Club Gold Cup (see page 17). Eight years then passed before the next meeting between two Kentucky Derby winners. The occasion in 1987 was the Breeders' Cup Classic, now worth $1,350,000 to the winner and the world's richest horse race; it produced a contest worthy of its billing.

Ferdinand, owned by Mrs Elizabeth Keck and trained by Charlie Whittingham, was a four-year-old who had won the Kentucky Derby in 1986; second by two and a quarter lengths was Bold Arrangement, sent over from Newmarket by Clive Brittain to become the first ever British-trained runner in the race. Alysheba, a year younger, had lifted the Derby and the Preakness earlier in 1987. He was trained by Jack Van Berg, who had won more races than any trainer in history and whose Gate Dancer had been beaten a head by Wild Again in the 1984 Classic and the same distance by Proud Truth in the 1985 running. Jack Van Berg deserved a change of luck, but Ferdinand's performances earlier in 1987 (he had won the Hollywood Gold Cup and the Cabrillo and Goodwood Handicaps – proved that he had trained on into a magnificent four-year-old. Pitch him against a horse who had taken two legs of the Triple Crown, and you have one of the most eagerly awaited races of the decade.

Breeders' Cup Day saw a crowd of 57,734 packed into Hollywood Park for racing's answer to the Superbowl or the World Series, to be thrilled by a succession of top-class races: Miesque scooted away from her field to win the Mile, and Theatrical and the Arc winner Trempolino fought out a stirring finish in the Turf. But for most of the crowd the final event on the card, the ten-furlong Classic, was the high point of the day.

There were twelve runners. Ferdinand was favourite at evens, with Alysheba 36–10. Skywalker, who had won the race in 1986, started at 83–10, and a long-priced outsider at 88–1 was the English raider Bold Arrangement, who in 1987 was not showing the form which the previous year had included his adventurous bid for the Kentucky Derby. There were really only two horses in it, and both of these outstanding performers enjoyed connections from the very first rank of the sport: Ferdinand trained by Whittingham and ridden by Bill Shoemaker, Alysheba trained by Jack Van Berg and ridden by Chris McCarron. Ferdinand was conceding his younger rival four pounds. It would be a classic confrontation.

The early pace was made by Candi's Gold and Judge Angelucci, and while these two outsiders vied for the lead Shoemaker and McCarron were content to sit in behind and manoeuvre themselves into positions from

## Breeders' Cup Classic

Hollywood Park
1¼ miles
21 November 1987

| 1 Ferdinand | W. Shoemaker | evens fav. |
| 2 Alysheba | C. McCarron | 36–10 |
| 3 Judge Angelucci | E. Delahoussaye | 169–10 |

*Also ran:* Candi's Gold (4th), Cryptoclearance, Good Command, Nostalgia's Star, He's A Saros, Gulch, Afleet, Bold Arrangement, Skywalker

12 ran

Winner owned by Mrs E. Keck, trained by C. Whittingham

*Distances:* nose, 1¼ lengths

*Ferdinand (pink cap) starts his stretch run, but Alysheba (no. 9) comes at him. Just short of the wire Alysheba is less than half a length down, but Ferdinand holds on.*

which to launch a run coming off the home turn. Going down the back stretch Ferdinand effortlessly moved up to within striking distance of the front pair; McCarron, six lengths further back on Alysheba, was in no hurry. The speed horses were still in front with a quarter of a mile to go, but once in the home stretch Ferdinand went for the wire, wresting the lead from Judge Angelucci at the one-sixteenth pole. Meanwhile Alysheba had engaged top gear and was starting to motor along the stretch on the stands side.

This was the essence of a great race: two Hall of Fame trainers, two of the finest jockeys riding, two brave and brilliant horses — a magnificent duel. McCarron went for his whip while Shoemaker refrained from applying any punishment to Ferdinand — 'He's not a whip horse.' But the blinkered head of Alysheba was gaining with every stride and the three-year-old seemed certain to overhaul the four-year-old as the two powered towards the line. With a hundred yards to go Ferdinand still had his nose in front but Alysheba looked sure to get up. McCarron put his whip down and pushed away with his hands. Shoemaker, on the rails, waved his whip out to the right. Both horses ran on unflinching, and they went under the wire clamped together.

Neither jockey knew who had won, and as they rode back to await the result of the photo they made an arrangement to 'save' $10,000 — the winning jockey would give the loser that amount from his percentage of the prize money.

It was Shoemaker who had to fork out, for the photograph showed that Ferdinand had stayed in front by a nose. Sheer dogged determination had kept him there, as the beaten jockey conceded: 'Ferdinand just kept digging in as my horse was getting to him. He was very game at the finish.'

But Alysheba's day would come. On Breeders' Cup Day 1988 at Churchill Downs he beat Seeking The Gold to give Jack Van Berg his first Turf Classic. Not before time.

# SPECIAL CARGO, LETTOCH AND DIAMOND EDGE

*Whitbread Gold Cup*
*Sandown Park, 28 April 1984*

*At the last fence Lettoch (left) and Plundering are together, with Diamond Edge (right) just behind and Special Cargo (black cap) still well behind.*

❛ *I just hope he still thinks he's won* ❜

The sight of a Whitbread Gold Cup field attacking the fences along the far side at Sandown Park is one of the most exhilarating that racing has to offer. And as the leaders in the 1984 race made for the three jumps close together at the far end of that straight – popularly known as the Railway Fences – the crowds packed into Sandown's modern grandstand for the course's most popular race on a wonderfully sunny spring day were seeing a more than ordinarily gripping contest unfold.

Several intriguing possibilities were still live. If top weight Diamond Edge, bounding along in front and treating the fences with the cavalier disdain which made him one of the most exciting chasers of recent memory, were to hold on to his lead not only would he give his jockey the perfect retirement present – this was Bill Smith's last ride – but he would bring himself two records. At thirteen he would be the oldest winner of this great race and, with the 1979 and 1981 runnings to his credit, would be the only horse

ever to have won it three times. A leg injury had kept him off the track for nearly two years until an encouraging recent run at the Cheltenham Festival, but he was showing all his old zest as he sprang over the Railway Fences and started on the long right-hand turn towards the Pond Fence – three from home – and the straight.

In close attendance was Ashley House. Were he or his stable-companion Lettoch to lift the prize, their trainer Michael Dickinson would be champion trainer for the third time in his fourth and last season handling jumpers. Ashley House's previous race had seen him beaten a neck at Cheltenham by Plundering, and as the same horse now went past the tiring Ashley House on the bend another possibility seemed ever more real – that Fred Winter, Plundering's trainer, would add the £25,472 first prize to his season's total and pip Dickinson for the trainers' title. But Dickinson's Lettoch, who had been brought to a halt by a fallen horse at the third fence and had forfeited at least twenty

The official photo-finish print: the distances were a short head and the same.

lengths, had gradually made up the lost ground and was now well in contention. There was still all to play for.

One possibility which at the Pond Fence was looking increasingly remote was that Special Cargo would give the Queen Mother her most valuable victory as an owner and in the process bring trainer Fulke Walwyn – also the handler of Diamond Edge – a seventh win in the race. Eleven-year-old Special Cargo, a good chaser on his day, had been off the course for two years with severe leg trouble. A new veterinary technique for damaged tendons in horses, carbon fibre implants, had been applied, and Special Cargo had advertised its efficacy by winning three races since his comeback in February, including two at Sandown Park (where he had never been beaten): the Horse and Hound Grand Military Gold Cup and the Alanbrooke Memorial Handicap Chase, in which he had worn down Plundering near the finish after having been under the whip a long way out. Now he was under pressure

again, and this time all the urgings of jockey Kevin Mooney seemed unable to bring Special Cargo into a challenging position.

The leaders straightened up towards the second last. Lettoch and Plundering had taken over from Diamond Edge but Smith had seemed to be giving the old horse a breather and he was not out of it yet. Special Cargo, six lengths adrift, apparently was. After the penultimate fence Diamond Edge was making no significant impression on the leaders, and as Plundering on the near side and Lettoch on the far side came to the last the alternatives seemed to be straightforward – Lettoch or Plundering, Michael Dickinson or Fred Winter. They took off together and landed together and made off up the hill with very little between them. Then Diamond Edge, who had been about two lengths behind at the last fence, started to rally. The very last ride of Bill Smith's career was becoming the most memorable, and as he urged Diamond Edge to go for the gap between Plundering and Lettoch he found a

*Special Cargo is led in.*

OPPOSITE *Acclaim for Desert Orchid after his victory in the 1989 Tote Cheltenham Gold Cup.*

willing response from his old friend. Three brave horses at full stretch and going for the line set off wild excitement in the grandstand, where few noticed that a fourth actor was about to appear on the scene. Mooney's encouragement had at last roused a renewed effort from Special Cargo, who now, in his element on the Sandown hill, found enough of a second wind to stage a last-gasp surge up the far side. Meanwhile, halfway up the run-in, Diamond Edge had pushed a neck in front of his younger rivals and for a moment, as Plundering weakened, looked about to gain a famous victory. Then Lettoch found hidden reserves of courage and came back to head Diamond Edge, but even as he did so Special Cargo flew by them on the outside and the three went past the post together.

To most spectators it was clear that Diamond Edge had not held on, but had Special Cargo got up? Kevin Mooney thought he had, and gave a victory salute as television commentator Graham Goode put into words the feeling of anyone who had seen

that finish: 'You'd have to travel a million miles to see a better race.' The photo finish showed that Special Cargo had beaten Lettoch by a short head, with Diamond Edge another short head back in third. Plundering was a length and a half back in fourth.

Delirious scenes followed in the winners' enclosure when the horses were led in, for most of those present were aware that they had just witnessed as near perfect a horse race as you could get, and – given all the different possibilities which the race had contained – a win for the Queen Mother was the ideal result. Yet it was a result tinged with sadness, for three fine chasers had given their all and two had been beaten. Diamond Edge had come so close to setting the seal on an extraordinary comeback, but Bill Smith needed no sympathy: he knew that on his last ride he taken a leading role in something very special. Nor did Cath Walwyn, wife of the victorious trainer, forget her husband's other charge Diamond Edge: 'I just hope he still thinks he won.'

# SECRETARIAT

*Belmont Stakes*
*Belmont Park, 9 June 1973*

*Secretariat hammers clear of his rivals . . .*

❡ *He could not have moved faster if he had fallen off the grandstand roof* ❡

To portray a race which beggars description we may enlist the help of the official chart of the 1973 Belmont Stakes:

> *SECRETARIAT sent up along the inside to vie for the early lead with SHAM to the backstretch, disposed of that one after going three-quarters, drew off at will rounding the far turn and was under a hand ride from Turcotte to establish a record in a tremendous performance.*

Or, to put it another way: this was probably the greatest display of individual brilliance provided by any racehorse in the modern era.

Secretariat was a giant in physique as well as performance. When he was fully grown to 16.2 hands his girth was measured at seventy-six inches, and it was estimated that his heart weighed between fourteen and seventeen pounds. This tremendous engine powered a racing machine which would produce a twenty-five foot stride at full gallop. And his power had been apparent from his earliest days. When Penny Tweedy, manager of the Meadow Stud in Virginia where Secretariat was born, first saw him as a foal she described him in her notebook with one word which he was to cause to be uttered a million times: 'Wow!'

The Meadow Stud had been founded by Mrs Tweedy's father Christopher Chenery,

*... and is led back in triumph.*

a breeder with a particular enthusiasm for the stallion Bold Ruler but less enthusiastic about the fees he commanded. So Chenery struck a novel deal with Bold Ruler's owner Ogden Phipps whereby Chenery would send two mares to the stallion annually and the two men would toss a coin for ownership of the foals, the winner having first choice and the loser that privilege the following year – thus the tossing of the coin would be enacted every other year. Ill health had caused Chenery's retirement from active involvement in the stud by the time the 1969 ritual took place, and it was Mrs Tweedy who lost that year's toss to Ogden Phipps. So in 1970 she had first choice – which was no choice at all, as only one of the

two mares that year was pregnant. The mare was Somethingroyal and the offspring, a bright red chestnut colt with three white stockings born in the early hours of 30 March 1970, was Secretariat.

The colt was put into training with Lucien Laurin and ran throughout his career in the colours of the Meadow Stable. In his first race on 4 July 1972 he finished fourth – the worst placing he ever recorded – after having been severely interfered with by another runner. But he finished first in his next eight races, and though he was disqualified after winning the Champagne Stakes he won the Futurity at Belmont Park and the Laurel Futurity. After winding up his juvenile campaign with a facile success in the Garden

State Stakes he was voted Horse of the Year.

Christopher Chenery died in January 1973 and the following month it was announced that Secretariat had been syndicated for stud purposes for the then world record sum of $6,080,000 in order to provide funds to meet taxes on the Chenery estate. Before long the thirty-two investors who had each paid $190,000 a share knew that they had a bargain, for Secretariat showed that he had trained on with an easy victory at Aqueduct in March. He then equalled the track record when winning the Gotham Stakes but suffered a shock defeat in the Wood Memorial, coming third to his stable-companion Angle Light: it transpired that a boil had infected his mouth just before the race.

Next came the Kentucky Derby, where he would be opposed by Sham, runner-up in the Wood Memorial and one of the best horses in California. Some journalists thought that Sham would have the measure of 'Big Red' – Secretariat had taken over Man O' War's nickname – but their heresy was emphatically punished as Secretariat came home two and a half lengths in front in a time which smashed the track record set by Northern Dancer nine years earlier (see pages 46–7). Secretariat handed out similar treatment to Sham in the Preakness, winning by the same margin after running at the rear of the field and then bearing down on his opponents like a wolf on the fold once jockey Ron Turcotte had given the horse his head.

Secretariat was now a national hero, all the more feted for the distraction his exploits provided from the unfolding drama of Watergate. Within the same week he was the cover illustration not only on *Sports Illustrated* but also on *Time* and *Newsweek*. The journalists rhapsodized about his physique and his impact. 'He has a neck like a buffalo, a back as broad as a sofa,' wrote *Time*. For *Newsweek*, 'he produces a breathtaking explosion that leaves novices and hardened horsemen alike convinced that, for one of those moments that seldom occur in any sport, they have witnessed genuine greatness.' For the New York *Post* he was the dream of every horse-player, 'the apparently unflawed hunk of beauty and beast that they

search for doggedly in the racing charts every day, and never seem to find'.

The Triple Crown had not been won since Citation had performed the feat a quarter of a century ago, but Secretariat was not seriously expected to be troubled by his four opponents in the Belmont Stakes, and he went off the 10–1 on favourite. The luckless Sham was a shade over 5–1, and the other three were unconsidered. A crowd of nearly 70,000 sweltered in ninety-degree heat as the complete outsider Twice A Prince was blindfolded for entry into the starting gate, and meanwhile Ron Turcotte was constructing a last-minute plan. He had noticed that Sham had not moved easily during the warm-up, so he 'decided to deliver Secretariat's knockout punch early'.

He did just that, and as the starting gates crashed open Secretariat's handsome head, clad in those distinctive blue and white check blinkers, shot out like a bullet from the inside berth. Laffit Pincay on Sham was taken aback by this surprise tactic and immediately gave chase. For two furlongs Secretariat and Sham hammered up the stretch towards the clubhouse turn, and the time at the first quarter drew unbelieving gasps from the crowd – 23.6 seconds, an absurd pace for a twelve-furlong race. They would surely burn each other out if they kept it up, but keep it up they did, and round the clubhouse turn they were neck and neck, with Sham momentarily pushing his head to the front. The time at half a mile was 46.2. Now they were into the back stretch, and with the other three horses already beaten off Secretariat and Sham slammed along towards halfway. But after six furlongs flat out Secretariat incredibly seemed to find another gear, and he started to build a clear advantage as Sham's gallant effort took its toll. Sham quickly fell away, leaving Turcotte and 'Big Red' in splendid isolation. According to the official chart the runners were 'against wind in backstretch', but if the wind had any sense it would have smartly got out the way as Secretariat gusted towards the home turn. He was rapidly increasing his lead, and was seven lengths up by the time the mile had been completed in 1 minute 34.2.

Despite doubts about his stamina it

*Secretariat in his paddock at Claiborne Farm.*

seemed inconceivable that Secretariat would not now go on to win, but after that extraordinary early pace it also seemed inconceivable that he he could keep up his furious gallop – especially as the other runners were now way behind and he had no spur of competition to keep him up to his work. But with two furlongs to run the lead had increased to twenty lengths and his time was 1 minute 59 seconds: he had travelled ten furlongs faster than he had done in his record-breaking Kentucky Derby, and he still had a quarter of a mile to go! As Turcotte steered Secretariat into the home stretch he caught a glimpse of the fraction times displayed on the infield tote board and realized that the track record was there for the taking. Cramming himself down onto the horse's neck and shortening the reins, he pushed Secretariat out, and still the horse had more to give. At the turn into the straight he was twenty-eight lengths clear, and to whoops of delight from the packed stands he barrelled home. At the wire he had won by thirty-one lengths from Twice A Prince.

He had won; but the performance was not over yet, for it took Turcotte over a furlong to pull the horse up, and despite the best efforts of his jockey to slow him down he was clocked for thirteen furlongs at under the world record. No wonder the great racing writer Charlie Hatton was led to observe: 'He could not have moved faster if he had fallen off the grandstand roof.'

Secretariat ran six more times, and was beaten twice – by Onion in the Whitney Stakes (after which he was found to be suffering from a virus) and by Prove Out in the Woodward Stakes. But Onion was well and truly pickled when they next met in the Marlboro Cup and finished fourth, Secretariat beating his stable-mate Riva Ridge (winner of the Kentucky Derby and the Belmont Stakes in 1972) in a world record time for nine furlongs. In the final phase of his career 'Big Red' also won the Arlington Invitational, the Man O' War Stakes (on grass) and the Canadian International Turf Championship at Woodbine. On his retirement to Claiborne Farm in Kentucky, where he died in October 1989, he had won sixteen of his twenty-one races for earnings of $1,316,808.

There is a more telling statistic to indicate the hold which Secretariat exerted on the American public. After the Belmont Stakes some 5617 winning tote tickets on the horse – value $14,597 – were not cashed. They were being kept as mementos.

**Belmont Stakes**

Belmont Park
1¹/₂ miles
9 June 1973

| 1 Secretariat | R. Turcotte | 1–10 fav. |
| 2 Twice A Prince | B. Baeza | 173–10 |
| 3 My Gallant | A. Cordero | 124–10 |

*Also ran:* Pvt. Smiles (4th), Sham

5 ran

Winner owned by Meadow Stable, trained by L. Laurin

*Distances:* 31 lengths, ¹/₂ length

# BROWN JACK

*Queen Alexandra Stakes*
*Ascot, 22 June 1934*

*Brown Jack comes home two
lengths clear of Solatium.*

❛ *Ascot or no Ascot, they
went mad* ❜

When the racing public takes a horse to its heart every contest in which that horse takes part is potentially a great race, and no Flat racer in Britain has ever enjoyed such popularity as Brown Jack. Usually ridden by the adored Steve Donoghue, Brown Jack became a national institution, and appropriately his true domain was the nation's most famous meeting, Royal Ascot, where he won for seven consecutive years. The greatest of his races there, the moment of the true apotheosis of Brown Jack, was the 1934 Queen Alexandra Stakes.

Bred in Ireland, Brown Jack had first changed hands as a yearling for £110, being sold on the following year (after having been gelded) for £275 to the Irish trainer Charlie Rogers. Fat, lazy and lethargic, Brown Jack came last in his first race, at Navan in May

1927, but then began to show promise, and was sold to Wroughton trainer Aubrey Hastings (who was looking for a National Hunt prospect for Major Harold Wernher) for £750 plus a contingency of £50 if he ever won a race: by the end of his career he had won twenty-five. His hurdling debut in Britain came at Bournemouth in September 1927, and by the following spring he had become such an accomplished hurdler that he started 4–1 third favourite for the second running of the Champion Hurdle. He won it by one and a half lengths.

Before the Champion, Brown Jack's trainer Hastings had asked Steve Donoghue, then approaching the end of a riding career in which he had dominated the jockeys' championship during and following the First World War, whether he thought Brown Jack might win on the Flat. After the race Donoghue gave his verdict: 'Yes, he'll win on the Flat, and I'll ride him.' Brown Jack won the Goodwood Cup, the Ebor Handicap, the Doncaster Cup and the Chester Cup, but it was at Royal Ascot that he really established his legend. He won the Ascot Stakes in 1928 and though beaten a short head in the same race the following year, he won later in that meeting the race which he was to make his own, the Queen Alexandra Stakes – at two and three quarter miles the longest Flat race run in Britain. Brown Jack and Donoghue won the race six years in succession, and the appreciation which their performances at Ascot and elsewhere engendered in the racing public and then in a wider audience gradually developed into a profound love for the horse. When it became known that Brown Jack was in the habit of sharing his lad Alfie Garratt's lunch of bread and cheese, his admirers sent him food parcels of all sorts of varieties of cheese – the horse, though, did not have expensive tastes and ate only the cheapest American cheddar.

By 1934 Brown Jack, now trained at Wroughton by Ivor Anthony following the retirement of Aubrey Hastings, was ten years old, and that year's Queen Alexandra Stakes was to be his last race. A huge crowd on the final day of the Royal Meeting was willing him on, and the atmosphere was tingling as Donoghue rode him out for the Queen Alexandra. He faced eight rivals, including his

## Queen Alexandra Stakes

Ascot
2 mile 6 furlongs 85 yards
22 June 1934

| | | |
|---|---|---|
| 1 Brown Jack | S. Donoghue | 6–4 fav. |
| 2 Solatium | J. Caldwell | 100–8 |
| 3 Dark Dew | W. Johnstone | 10–1 |

*Also ran:* Harinero (4th), Nitsichin, Mail Fist, Our Hope, Loosestrife, Benskin

9 ran

Winner owned by Sir H. Wernher, trained by I. Anthony

*Distances:* 2 lengths, 6 lengths

*Brown Jack and Steve Donoghue.*

pacemaker Mail Fist, ridden by Steve Donoghue's son Pat, and a very useful stayer in Solatium, to whom he was conceding eight pounds and six years. As the runners cantered to the start – right at the far end of the Ascot straight – clapping and cheering broke out from the pent-up masses, and Donoghue senior, going down alongside his son, asked him to 'Pull back, Pat, let the old horse have his day.'

Mail Fist duly made the running, with Brown Jack about five lengths behind as the field came past the stands on the first circuit. But with more than a mile to go the pacemaker weakened, and Steve Donoghue overtook his son, nearly putting him over the rails in the process. By the time the straight was reached Brown Jack and Solatium had drawn clear of the rest of the field, and there ensued a famous tussle, well described by Donoghue in his autobiography *Donoghue Up!*:

*We battled along side by side for the best part of a hundred yards, and I know people on the stands must have been thinking that old Jack had at last met his match, but he had not...*
*Here he was racing in the last race of his career. I had lost my whip some distance before the end of the race... He knew me and he knew the occasion and he battled on splendidly, but as sure as my name is what it is, I am certain that the old rogue was laughing at me for having dropped my whip and I know that he enjoyed giving me that fright. Just as he had done every time before, he pricked his ears as he approached the post and did his little comic dance – he always did this when he won – as he passed it.*

Laughing or not, Brown Jack had forged ahead in the final furlong to win by two lengths, and the scenes which followed are more famous than the race itself, as delirious racegoers fought their way to the unsaddling enclosure to give vent to their idolatry of this great old horse. Their hero milked the applause, pausing at the entrance to the winner's circle to ensure (as some witnesses liked to think) that all his admirers were in place, before walking in to as great an ovation as any heard on a British racecourse. 'Never will I forget the roar of that crowd as long as I live,' wrote Donoghue of the post-race hysteria; 'Ascot or no Ascot, they went mad. I have never seen so many hats flung in the air, and I have never heard such shrieks of joy in my life. All my six Derbys faded before the reception that was awaiting Jack and myself as we set out to return to weigh-in. I don't think I was ever so happy in my life as I was at that moment.'

Trainer Ivor Anthony had not witnessed his charge's triumph. So nervous was he that he had spent the race sitting alone under a tree in the paddock until the cheering assured him that his horse had won.

At every traffic jam on the journey back to Wroughton that evening the police waved the horsebox through when they saw the words which had been painted on the windscreen – BROWN JACK.

# DESERT ORCHID

*At the last fence Desert Orchid (left) is just behind Yahoo...*

*It was just sheer guts that got us home*

The rain was hammering on the roof of Richard Burridge's car as he arrived at Cheltenham racecourse shortly before 10 a.m. He parked, got out of the car, and just stood there in the downpour, laughing.

Six hours later Desert Orchid, in whom Burridge owned the major share, was due to run in the Cheltenham Gold Cup, and after month upon month of public debate about whether the nation's favourite racehorse should take his place in the season's most prestigious steeplechase, it now seemed that the English climate would have the last laugh. The first two days of the 1989 Cheltenham National Hunt Festival had already provided a representative sample of Cotswold spring weather: the Tuesday had been wet, cold and windy, the Wednesday bright, warm and sunny. In the early hours of Thursday – Gold Cup day – thick snow started fall-ing on the surrounding hills and then on the racecourse. This turned to sleet and then incessant heavy rain, and by the time Burridge parked his car parts of the track were under water. How would Desert Orchid cope with such conditions? Should he be withdrawn from the race? Would the day's racing be allowed to go ahead anyway? After all the preparation, all the agonizing about whether to go for the Gold Cup, here was the course being bombarded with rain before Burridge's very eyes, and every drop was diminishing the chances of his horse. Laugh? It was enough to make him weep.

Desert Orchid had taken his hold on the hearts of the British public over several years of spectacular performance. A striking grey gelding (who had become whiter as he aged), he was a superbly bold jumper who liked to run his races from the front and appeared to hate being passed: time and

*... but he claws his way back ...*

again a rival would come to head him at or after the last fence, only to be seen off up the run-in. By Gold Cup day 1989 he had won nineteen races over fences (in addition to seven over hurdles) and was the best chaser in training by a considerable margin. In the early part of his steeplechasing career he had raced mainly over trips of up to two and a half miles, and in December 1986 he had started a 16–1 outsider for the King George VI Rank Chase at Kempton Park, as it was widely held that he would find the three-mile trip too far; but he skipped over the fences and galloped a high-class field into the ground. Desert Orchid the staying chaser had arrived. In April 1988 he powered up the Sandown Park hill to win the Whitbread Gold Cup over three miles five furlongs, and throughout the 1988–9 season had seemed to be getting even better. He had won the King George again and put up memorable

displays in handicaps at Ascot (beating Panto Prince by a head in a thrilling finish to a two-mile chase to emphasize again his extraordinary versatility) and at Sandown Park (beating Pegwell Bay, to whom he was conceding eighteen pounds, by three-quarters of a length, fighting his way back into the lead close home after being headed).

If Desert Orchid were so obviously the best chaser around, why all the fuss about running him in the most important chase? It was argued that he did not like Cheltenham; the going for the Gold Cup was likely to be soft (or worse), which would not suit him; and the race itself puts demands on a horse which might prove more than Desert Orchid, with so many other factors militating against him, could readily withstand.

Yet the Cheltenham Gold Cup was *the* race. If Desert Orchid were to prove himself a chaser in the very top bracket he had to

*... and at the line Simon Sherwood punches the air in triumph.*

win it, and eventually it was decided that he would take his chance.

But would there be a race at all? Early on that sodden Thursday morning there was considerable doubt. There was still standing water on the course when the Stewards went out for an inspection at noon, but they decided that racing could go ahead.

The crowd of more than 51,000 people who were flocking to Cheltenham were under no illusions. These were extreme conditions, and few would have been surprised had Richard Burridge and his co-owners decided with trainer David Elsworth that Desert Orchid could not be risked. The grey's jockey Simon Sherwood (who had first ridden the horse in the 1986 King George and had never been beaten on him in seven rides since) returned from riding in the first race to report that the horses were managing to get through the ground, and it was decided that he would run – though Sherwood was under instructions to pull Desert Orchid up after the first two fences if he was clearly not enjoying himself.

Not all eyes were on Desert Orchid, for among his twelve opponents were some of

the best staying chasers around. The two horses most fancied to upset the grey were the Irish challenger Carvill's Hill, a horse of immense promise but running in only his fifth steeplechase and prone to jumping errors, and Ten Plus, who had won on his last four outings and was bidding to give trainer Fulke Walwyn his fifth win in the race. Two previous winners were each attempting to become the first horse since L'Escargot in 1971 to win the Gold Cup twice: Charter Party, winner in 1988, and The Thinker, victorious in the 1987 running.

The bookmakers thought that Desert Orchid could not win in such conditions and pushed his odds out to 7–2 before shortening him up again to his starting price of 5–2. Carvill's Hill at 5–1 was marginally preferred to Ten Plus at 11–2, then came Welsh National winner Bonanza Boy on 15–2, the same price as The Thinker. Among the outsiders was Yahoo, trained by John Edwards and ridden by Tom Morgan: he loved the mud and attracted some shrewd each-way bets.

In the early stages of the race the front-running Desert Orchid was pressed by Ten Plus, with Charter Party, Bonanza Boy, Slalom and Yahoo in close attendance. At the sixth fence the good young chaser Golden Freeze fell, and at the next Carvill's Hill paid the price of a jumping error and crashed to the floor. Meanwhile at the front of the field Desert Orchid continued to take the runners along, though he was not liking the ground and not jumping with his wonted spring-heeled agility. They came down the hill, and at the fence before the turn into the straight The Thinker suffered a heavy fall. This race was taking its toll.

Closely bunched, the survivors came past the stands with a circuit still to race, and now the tall, handsome form of Ten Plus was pressing Desert Orchid, with the grey's stable-companion Cavvies Clown making a significant forward move from the rear. They made the uphill turn out into the country again, and soon Ten Plus had taken the lead. ('It gave my horse a bit of a rest,' said Simon Sherwood later: 'Glad to let someone else do the hard work!') The conditions had exacted their price, and approaching the top of the hill only seven horses were left in the race with any sort of chance: Ten Plus led from Desert Orchid, then came Yahoo and Charter Party, the rallying Bonanza Boy, Ballyhane and Slalom. But Slalom fell six fences from home, and then Kevin Mooney on Ten Plus committed himself, for he knew that his horse would be staying on at the end of the race. But how would the inexperienced Ten Plus jump under pressure? Four from home, with the two most difficult fences on the course coming up, this was the time to find out. Ten Plus jumped the fourth last cleanly but Desert Orchid hit it hard, throwing Simon Sherwood back in his saddle, and for a few moments it looked as if Ten Plus had the measure of the grey. They careered down the hill to the third last, and here tragedy struck: Ten Plus failed to get high enough, fell and broke his near-hind pastern. Within minutes he had been destroyed.

That fatal fall left the race between Desert Orchid and Yahoo, who had made relentless progress on the second circuit: he had now slipped through on the inside and was staying on doggedly in the heavy ground. As the two turned into the straight to face up to the second last fence there was no doubt that it was the outsider who was going the better. At the second last he was a length up and Desert Orchid was clearly tiring, but with the huge crowd urging him on he was not finished with, and coming to the final fence he started to drag himself back. Sherwood resisted the temptation to ask his exhausted mount for something spectacular at the last and allowed him to pop over it; on landing he was still half a length down. Yahoo had the rails to guide him up that final climb to the winning post and still looked the winner, for Desert Orchid was wandering towards the stands rails and risked losing vital ground. But a few smacks from Sherwood's whip brought a response from the grey which set Cheltenham on a roar. Halfway up the run-in Desert Orchid had brought himself level with Yahoo, but even as he did so he veered to the left towards his rival – 'It was his way of telling Yahoo to shove off,' said Sherwood. The jockey yanked him to the right and pushed him through the final few yards as the soaked but exalted crowd went berserk with excitement. At the line he had won by a length and a half.

For the second time in four years complete pandemonium reigned as the winner of the Cheltenham Gold Cup came back past the stands. Whether the ecstasy surpassed that of Dawn Run's victory in 1986 (see pages 123–5) is beside the point: the reception afforded to Desert Orchid was without doubt one of the all-time great scenes of National Hunt racing. Horse and jockey were mobbed all the way back to the unsaddling enclosure, where the euphoric bedlam continued for fully half an hour before Desert Orchid was led away.

A year later he would be back in that unsaddling enclosure after the Gold Cup, but this time in the place for the third horse, for in 1990 he was beaten in much more clement conditions by the 100–1 outsider Norton's Coin (see pages 118–20). No matter. Nor would it matter that the form experts would declare that Desert Orchid had run well below his best in beating Yahoo by one and a half lengths. This was a moment of sheer racing emotion set off by the horse's raw courage; as Cheltenham eventually regained its composure those most closely involved gave their reactions, and owners, trainer and jockey all paid tribute to their horse's determination: 'It was just sheer guts that got us home, and both Dessie and I were absolutely knackered,' reported Sherwood.

But for all the words which would be spoken and written about this famous race, one gesture in its immediate aftermath sums up why it was so special, how even those whom Desert Orchid had pushed aside to reach his moment of glory could acknowledge his greatness. Tom Morgan had ridden a brilliant race on Yahoo, and his enterprise in pushing on at the final bend had so nearly paid off. He had been beaten, but he would add his own eloquent tribute to his conqueror. As the two horses turned to walk back to unsaddle, Morgan leant over from Yahoo and affectionately patted Desert Orchid's head.

**Tote Cheltenham Gold Cup**

Cheltenham
3¼ miles
16 March 1989

| 1 | Desert Orchid | S. Sherwood | 5–2 fav. |
| 2 | Yahoo | T. Morgan | 25–1 |
| 3 | Charter Party | R. Dunwoody | 14–1 |

*Also ran:* Bonanza Boy (4th), West Tip, Ballyhane, Carvill's Hill, Golden Freeze, Ten Plus, The Thinker, Slalom, Pegwell Bay, Cavvies Clown

13 ran

Winner owned by R. Burridge, trained by D. Elsworth

*Distances:* 1½ lengths, 8 lengths

# MAN O' WAR

❦ *The mostest hoss that
ever was* ❧

On the edge of the Kentucky Horse
Park, just outside the city of Lexington, stands a huge bronze statue of a horse set on a granite plinth. The
plaque situated at the entrance to the tree-
lined path leading to this shrine explains that
this is the grave of Man O' War. He deserves
such a memorial. One of the greatest horses
the world has ever seen, he was beaten only
once in two seasons of competition. His run
against his solitary opponent John P. Grier in
the 1920 Dwyer Stakes was the hardest race
he ever had.

Man O' War was bred by August Belmont
II, chairman of the New York Jockey Club. In
1918, at the age of sixty-five, Belmont
decided to enlist in the US Army to join the
war in Europe (where he was given the job
of buying mules), and sold all his yearlings at
the sales at Saratoga. Man O' War (initially
named My Man O' War by Belmont's wife in
his honour) was sold for $5000 to Penn-
sylvania textile manufacturer Samuel Doyle
Riddle and put into training with Louis Feustel. The trainer had thought the yearling gan-
gling and ungainly, but Riddle was moved to
buy him as he thought he might have poten-
tial as a hunter.

Christened 'Big Red' on account of his
rich chestnut colour, Man O' War grew into
a magnificent looking two-year-old, with a
voracious appetite not only for food – he ate
twelve quarts of oats a day – but also for action, becoming almost impossible to res-

train. His first race was at Belmont on 6 June
1919, and after impressive trials he started
odds-on favourite. He obliged by six lengths.
Three days later he won again, and within
two months had clocked up six wins from
six races. In the Sanford Memorial at Saratoga on 13 August he met Harry Payne Whitney's Upset: an opponent who lived up to his
name by handing Man O' War the only defeat
of his life, beating him half a length. But Man
O' War had lost several lengths as one of the
worst sufferers from a straggling start and
had got boxed in: by the time his jockey
Johnny Loftus had switched him to the outside to make his challenge Upset was gone
beyond recall. Man O' War had been conceding fifteen pounds to Upset, and when
they met again ten days later the concession
was only five pounds: 'Big Red' took an easy
revenge, and went on to win the Hopeful
Stakes at Saratoga and the Belmont Futurity
to complete a two-year-old career of ten
runs and nine wins.

Samuel Riddle had his own views about
racing and did not enter Man O' War for the
Kentucky Derby, feeling that to run his colt
over ten furlongs so early in the season
would be detrimental to his future develop-
ment. But he won the Preakness (again beating Upset) and the Withers Stakes before
striding home twenty lengths ahead of his
single opponent Donnacona in the Belmont
Stakes. Then he sauntered through the Stuy-
vesant Handicap, the first of the three occasions in 1920 when Man O' War started at
odds of 100–1 on. (He never started at odds
against.)

His next race was the Dwyer Stakes, a
handicap at Aqueduct over nine furlongs. He
faced only one opponent, but John P. Grier
was a top-class horse, and in receipt of eighteen pounds would surely make a race of it.
Trained by James Rowe for Upset's owner
Whitney, the three-year-old John P. Grier
started at 7–2. Man O' War was 5–1 on.

Rumours had been circulating before the
race that Louis Feustel was not entirely
happy with his charge, but Man O' War
evinced no lack of readiness when he
appeared on the course: he was the show-
man, and like many great horses who
become the object of hero-worship he
played to the gallery, prancing along under

*Man O' War's grave and
monument at the Kentucky Horse
Park, Lexington, Kentucky.*

*Man O' War asserts and goes clear, leaving John P. Grier toiling in his wake.*

jockey Clarence Kummer, his regular rider since Johnny Loftus's licence had not been renewed. By contrast, John P. Grier went tamely to the start with jockey Eddie Ambrose; but once at the gate he became frisky, and with Man O' War eager to get on with it as usual the stage was set for an explosive race.

They left the gate like twin rockets, and though John P. Grier tried to take an early lead Man O' War would have none of it. He forced himself in front by half a length and stayed there. Down the back straight they charged, both at full tilt, and still 'Big Red' clung to his advantage. Then, halfway round the far turn, Ambrose tried to improve the Whitney colt's position and moved him up slightly, so that as they came into the home stretch Man O' War's advantage had shrunk to a neck. Now the weight difference would tell, and halfway up the stretch they were on even terms. For a fraction of a second John P. Grier seemed to be going the better, but then Kummer's whip slammed down on Man O' War, and the big horse was stung into a response, bounding forward to take a fresh advantage of half a length or more. So Ambrose brought his whip down harder and harder, again and again, and John P. Grier rallied to get back all but level. The reporter from the *New York Times* was caught up in the excitement: 'Men and women who are usually serene and dignified jumped up and down and waved arms frantically.' Quite right: this was no time for serenity, for with a hundred yards to run 'Big Red' was truly up

against it. As John P. Grier edged upsides Kummer gave Man O' War two more lashes with his whip. They were enough. With fifty yards to go the exhausted John P. Grier finally cracked. He could find no more, and stopped almost to nothing. Man O' War won by one and a half lengths.

'To more than 25,000 persons who witnessed the whirlwind battle of speed and stamina', wrote the *New York Times*, 'it provided a thrill such as is seldom experienced in any horse race no matter how close the finish may be ... The contestants had set such a dazzling pace from the very start that they seemed fairly to fly through space rather than to touch ground.' Jockey Clarence Kummer remarked that his horse 'ran a hard race, but he was not all in at the end'.

Man O' War was now the undisputed three-year-old champion, and for him the rest of the season was a glorious procession of victories. He won the Miller and the Travers, and beat his only rival by one hundred lengths in the Lawrence Realisation Stakes. Then, having taken the Jockey Club Stakes and the Potomac Handicap (in which he defeated that year's Kentucky Derby winner Paul Jones), he bade his farewell to the racecourse by beating Sir Barton, the 1919 Triple Crown winner, in an $80,000 match at Kenilworth Park, Canada.

'Big Red' spent most of his stud career at Faraway Farm in Kentucky, where Riddle restricted him to no more than twenty-five mares per season. By far the best of his offspring was War Admiral, the Triple Crown winner of 1937 whose famous match against Seabiscuit is described on pages 38–40, and he also sired the diminutive Battleship, winner of the Grand National in 1938.

On Man O' War's twenty-first birthday his owner sent him a cake bearing twenty-one candles, and when the great champion died at the age of thirty in 1947 he was laid in state in his box at Faraway Farm: his coffin was lined with silk in Riddle's black and gold racing colours. The most fitting epitaph comes from Will Harburt, the stallion man who looked after the horse for most of his stud career. Man O' War was simply 'the mostest hoss that ever was'.

**Dwyer Stakes**

Aqueduct
1 mile 1 furlong
10 July 1920

| | | |
|---|---|---|
| 1 Man O' War | C. Kummer | 1–5 fav. |
| 2 John P. Grier | E. Ambrose | 7–2 |

2 ran
Winner owned by Glen Riddle Farm, trained by L. Feustel

*Distance*: 2 lengths

# SHERGAR

*Irish Sweeps Derby*
*The Curragh, 27 June 1981*

*Shergar and Lester Piggott out for a stroll.*

Shergar was abducted from the Bally-many Stud in County Kildare on the night of 8 February 1983, a week before he was due to commence his second season as a stallion. He was never recovered, and it is assumed that his kidnappers – widely though not conclusively thought to be the IRA – killed the horse when they realized that their ransom demand of £2 million would not be met. This inanely bungled crime robbed the European bloodstock industry of the services of one of the very best horses of the post-war period. Had he been able to pass on to his progeny a fraction of his prodigious talent his imposing presence would have lived on through his offspring; as it is the memory of his fate will overshadow reminiscence of his racing career.

But what a career! At his best Shergar turned in devastating performances, and although his victory in the Derby at Epsom recorded the longest winning margin in the history of the race, for sheer domination of his rivals in a Classic the 1981 Irish Sweeps Derby saw Shergar at his very peak.

Owned and bred by the Aga Khan and trained at Newmarket by Michael Stoute, Shergar had run only twice as a two-year-old, winning the one-mile Kris Plate at Newbury and running second to Beldale Flutter in the William Hill Futurity at Doncaster. His first

appearance at three proclaimed him something out of the ordinary, his ten-length victory in the Guardian Classic Trial at Sandown Park putting him firmly into the Derby picture. Twelve lengths was the distance when he won the Chester Vase, and on Derby Day he started at 11–10 on, the hottest favourite since Sir Ivor in 1968. Not for a second did he look like losing, and after taking the lead on entering the straight went further and further away. His jockey Walter Swinburn gave him three or four smacks with the whip to keep him up to his work, and then eased him before the line, where the official winning distance was ten lengths. The previous longest winning distance in the Derby was that of Manna, eight lengths clear in 1925.

The Irish Derby reached its current status as one of the very top international races for three-year-olds when its prize money was boosted by an injection of cash through its connection with the Irish Sweeps in 1962 (in which year it was worth substantially more than its English equivalent). Since then it has become the natural target for the Epsom winner. None of those who had traipsed home in Shergar's wake at Epsom reopposed him, and only two of his eleven rivals at The Curragh looked capable of shaking him up. Kirtling, trained by Harry Wragg, had won the Dee Stakes at Chester by six lengths and the Gran Premio D'Italia in Milan, but he had been well beaten by Shergar at Sandown Park. Cut Above had won the White Rose Stakes at Ascot and looked a promising horse in the making: he started at 14–1, behind Shergar at 3–1 on and Kirtling at 12–1.

Walter Swinburn's suspension after the King Edward VII Stakes at Royal Ascot cost him the mount in the Irish Derby: his substitute was Lester Piggott, who had ridden Shergar in both his races as a two-year-old. The extremes of Lester Piggott in the saddle always made a wondrous sight. At one end of the scale of his remarkable skills was the powerhouse finish, the merciless rousting of his mount to effort of which it had not thought itself capable – Roberto in the Derby in 1972 or The Minstrel in the same race in 1977. At the other end was the Piggott in complete command, when only the

*He's only in an exercise canter!*

*An unruffled Shergar after the race.*

confidence oozing from every pore betrayed the fact that the motionless creature on the horse's back was a human being and not a statue – Nijinsky in the St Leger in 1970 or Sagaro in the Ascot Gold Cup in 1977. It was the latter Piggott who now turned in a virtuoso performance on Shergar, and never had the great jockey ridden a cooler race.

The going was good to firm, and Piggott was under instructions not to pressurize his mount unless it was truly necessary. It was not, but the tenderness with which he handled Shergar had to be seen to be believed. Tongue lolling out, the horse sauntered along in the early stages, and as the other jockeys got down to serious work with six furlongs to run Piggott's bottom disdainfully went higher into the air. As the runners came into the straight with about three furlongs to go Shergar was coasting. It was an extraordinary sight – all the runners in a major Classic except one being scrubbed along by their jockeys as the other runner, poking his tongue out contemptuously,

casually cantered along with them as if part of a different film being played at a slower speed. Shergar's rivals were not all moderate horses, but they may as well have been parking meters for all the difficulty he had in strolling past them when Lester Piggott decided that he may as well go on and win the race as television commentator Peter O'Sullevan enthused, 'He's only in an exercise canter!' Shergar, bouncing off the ground like a rocking horse, swishing his tail amiably and pricking his ears, scampered up the straight as Piggott glanced behind to his right and then his left as if looking for someone to talk to. The winning margin – four lengths from Cut Above – was significantly less than at Epsom, but Shergar had got there without any apparent effort whatsoever. To perform thus in a Classic was the mark of an exceptional horse.

Not far across the vast plain of The Curragh, the scene of Shergar's most telling triumph, is the Ballymany Stud, where he was last seen alive on 8 February 1983.

# RAIN LOVER

*Melbourne Cup*
*Flemington, 4 November 1969*

*Rain Lover (no. 2) and Alsop fight out the finish.*

The Melbourne Cup is always one of the great occasions of world racing, and on the first Tuesday of November every year a massive crowd flocks to Flemington, just outside Melbourne, for a social event which for Australians is Derby Day, Royal Ascot and the Kentucky Derby rolled into one. But in perverse contrast to the great races which crown those other meetings, the Melbourne Cup itself is not a race that pits the cream of the crop against each other on level terms, but a two-mile handicap. In 1969 a crowd of 85,600 sweltered on the hottest Cup day for twenty years (thirty women fainted in the heat) and the five-year-old Rain Lover became the first horse to win the race in successive years since Archer had won the first two runnings in 1861 and 1862.

Rain Lover's owner Clifford Reid had won the race in 1945 with his only previous run-

ner, Rainbird, and his brother Malcolm had owned the 1963 winner Gatum Gatum. Rain Lover, by Ribot's son Latin Lover (who had run sixth to Psidium in the 1961 Derby at Epsom), was first trained by Grahame Heagney, but when his handler moved to the USA after Rain Lover's three-year-old season the horse came under the care of Heagney's ex-foreman Mick Robins, a one-time coal miner who had broken the horse in and knew him well. Rain Lover had won once from four starts as a two-year-old and four times as a three-year-old, though one of his best performances in the 1967–8 season was finishing second in the SAJC St Leger to the filly Lowland. He would meet her again.

As a four-year-old he won the two-mile Adelaide Cup and was beaten about an inch by Lowland in the Craiglee Stakes; he also ran second to her in the Underwood Stakes at Caulfield, though he was unplaced in the

> *◀ Now they can all go and jump in the lake ▶*

Caulfield Cup. As a prelude to his first Melbourne Cup bid he won the Mackinnon Stakes at Flemington, and then lined up with twenty-five others for the Cup itself. Lowland (unplaced behind Rain Lover in the Mackinnon) was joint favourite with Arctic Coast, but after a very rough race Jim Johnson pushed Rain Lover clear of his field to win at 7–1. The eight lengths which he had to spare over his nearest rival Fileur equalled the longest winning distance in the Cup, and he broke the course record for two miles.

So why, a year later, did Rain Lover start at 8–1 to repeat the feat? Early in 1969 he had won three good races and come second to Lowland, giving her twelve pounds, in the Sydney Cup; and after his break for the Australian winter he returned to action, with wins in the Craiglee Stakes and the Underwood Stakes before going down by a half-head to Fileur in the Turnbull Stakes. But then he seemed to lose his form. He was fourth in the Caulfield Stakes, and in the Mackinnon Stakes on the opening day of the Melbourne Cup meeting was a disappointing fourth of five when even-money favourite. Big Philou, a narrowly beaten second in that race, vied for favouritism for the 1969 Melbourne Cup with Tails, who had won the Metropolitan and the Hotham Handicap, but Big Philou was sensationally withdrawn from the race forty minutes before the start, which threw the betting into turmoil and left the crowd of 85,600 bewildered. Only later did it emerge that the horse had been got at, and meanwhile the remaining twenty-three runners were saddled and paraded. In the absence of Big Philou, Tails started the 2–1 favourite; also preferred to Rain Lover in the betting were Fileur (11–2) and Nausori (6–1).

Rain Lover was carrying the hefty burden of nine stone seven pounds (joint top weight with General Command), but 'Jerky Jim' Johnson (so called because of his whip action), going for a rare third victory in the Cup, knew the horse well and did not try to restrain him. Rain Lover was in a prominent position from the off and was sent to the front a long way from home. Coming into the straight he still led, but the weight was beginning to anchor him and he could not assert himself as he had a year earlier under

nineteen pounds less. The four-year-old Alsop, like Rain Lover an 8–1 chance but carrying a burden two stone lighter, detached himself from the pursuers and took on the leader. He seemed to be going easily, and halfway up the straight had taken a narrow advantage, but Rain Lover was going for his place in history and had no intention of giving in tamely. He came back at Alsop and the two drove into the final furlong with nothing between them. Surely the weight difference would tell in favour of the younger horse, but Johnson asked Rain Lover for all his reserves of courage, and at the end of a gruelling race his mount found more. Responding to the jockey's urging, he scraped back into the lead just before the line and got the verdict by a head.

For Jim Johnson victory was especially sweet, as he had come in for much criticism of his riding of Rain Lover earlier in the season: 'I would have been booed off Flemington if I had lost, and my knockers would have said I had ridden another bad race. Now they can all go and jump in the lake.'

Rain Lover was the first horse this century to win the Melbourne Cup in successive years, and though the feat was repeated within the decade by Think Big (1974 and 1975), the 1969 running had produced one of the greatest races in the Cup's history.

Rain Lover continued to race during the early part of 1970, and when he was retired to stud that year was second only to Tulloch (see pages 90–1) in prize money won in Australia. His winnings of A$188,650 had come from a career record of seventeen wins, ten seconds and eight thirds in forty-six races.

## Melbourne Cup

Flemington
2 miles
4 November 1969

| 1 | Rain Lover | J. Johnson | 8–1 |
| 2 | Alsop | R. Setches | 8–1 |
| 3 | Ben Lomond | R. Lang | 9–1 |

*Also ran:* Lochcourt (4th), Swift General, Stay Fresh, Tails, Double Steel, Fileur, Ribottobir, Gnapur, Cyrano, General Command, Sir Kinsman, Astound, Wyscan, Debhel Boy, Terminal, Padtheway, The Sharper, Galleon King, Nausori, Hamua

23 ran

Winner owned by C. A. Reid, trained by M. L. Robins

*Distances:* head, 2 lengths

# TRIPTYCH

*Phoenix Champion Stakes*
*Phoenix Park, 6 September 1987*

> *She was a real character*

Triptych was the 'Iron Lady' of world racing in the 1980s. She ran in forty-one races – thirty-five of them Group or Grade One – in seven countries, and won fourteen times over five seasons; nine of her victories came in Group or Grade One events. Her total earnings were £1,589,089, of which just short of £1 million came in first-place money.

But the bare statistics, remarkable as they are, form only part of the Triptych story, and her lasting place in the affections of the racing public owes more to her remarkable toughness in contests at the very highest level, and the individuality of her way of running. She was her own horse.

Her achievements were so many and so various that it is impossible to single out one performance to represent the quintessential Triptych. Should it be the occasion in May 1985 when she became the first filly ever to win the Irish Two Thousand Guineas? Or the 1986 Dubai Champion Stakes – run that year on the July Course at Newmarket – when she showed a stunning turn of foot to defeat Celestial Storm less than two weeks after finishing a gallant third to Dancing Brave in the Prix de l'Arc de Triomphe (see pages 104–6)? Or the 1987 Coronation Cup, when she seemed unwilling to exert herself at all on the firm ground in the early stages but, coaxed into action by a sublimely sympathetic ride from Steve Cauthen, swept derisively past her rivals once she had decided to put her best foot forward? If we focus on the 1987 Phoenix Champion Stakes, it is because the prize of £238,839 was the largest single amount she won (and accounts for nearly a quarter of her first-place money), because it formed the middle leg of a remarkable treble which started with the Matchmaker International Stakes at York and ended with the Dubai Champion Stakes at Newmarket, and because the manner of her winning was so characteristic. When Triptych won the Phoenix Champion Stakes she was at the very height of her powers.

Triptych was a tall, occasionally rather ungainly filly. In her races she often held her head high, but this was no sign of irresolution, for she was as tough as a racehorse could be. This trait she inherited from her globe-trotting dam Trillion, second to

Alleged in the 1978 Prix de l'Arc de Triomphe, and with Riverman her sire it was no surprise that Alan Clore had to go to $2.15 million to secure her at the Keeneland Sales as a yearling in 1983. She was put into training with David Smaga in France and won two of her three races as a juvenile, including the Group One Prix Marcel Boussac at Longchamp. By the beginning of the 1985 season she had been moved to David O'Brien's stable in Ireland, and won the One Thousand Guineas Trial at Phoenix Park before embarking on a remarkable sequence of runs in Classic races: within the space of eight weeks she took part in the One Thousand Guineas at Newmarket (seventh to Oh So Sharp, beaten about four lengths), the Irish Two Thousand Guineas (won by two and a half lengths from Celestial Bounty), the Irish One Thousand Guineas (fifth to Al Bahathri when 7–4 favourite), the Oaks (second, beaten six lengths by Oh So Sharp) and the Irish Derby (fifth behind Law Society). She then had a short – and doubtless very welcome – break before running third to Commanche Run in the Benson and Hedges Gold Cup at York and unplaced behind the same horse in the Phoenix Champion Stakes. The season which had begun for her in April ended in late October with a third in the Rothmans International Stakes at Woodbine, Toronto.

By the start of the 1986 season she had spent some time with John Gosden in California (though she did not race for him) before returning to Europe to be trained in France by Patrick Biancone. She ran eleven times in five countries between 4 May (fourth in the Prix Ganay at Longchamp) and 23 November (eleventh in the Japan Cup in Tokyo). She was second to Saint Estephe in the Coronation Cup, second to Dancing Brave in the Eclipse Stakes, third to the same horse in both the King George VI and Queen Elizabeth Diamond Stakes at Ascot and the Prix de l'Arc de Triomphe, second to Shardari in the Matchmaker International Stakes (as the Benson and Hedges Gold Cup had now become), third to Park Express in the Phoenix Champion Stakes, and sixth in the Breeders' Cup Classic (on dirt). Besides the Champion Stakes at Newmarket she won La Coupe at Longchamp, the

only time all season that she ran in other than a Group One or Grade One event. 'Iron Lady' indeed!

In 1987 she got better. After victories in the Prix Ganay and the Coronation Cup she was third behind Mtoto and Reference Point in the Eclipse Stakes (see pages 48–9) and third to Reference Point in the King George. She then embarked on an attempt at the three great ten-furlong races of the season – the Matchmaker International, the Phoenix Champion, and the Dubai Champion.

Steve Cauthen (the eleventh jockey to ride her) had partnered her at York when she beat Ascot Knight, but at Phoenix Park she was reunited with Tony Cruz, who had

first had the mount on Triptych in the 1986 Dubai Champion Stakes and had won three of his seven races on her. There had been some worry that the ground might be too firm for her in Ireland, so she was declared for the Grosser Preis von Baden in Germany as a precaution: it would be a shame to deny her an outing that Sunday afternoon. But the Phoenix Park going was considered acceptable, and she travelled to Dublin as planned. Among her opponents were Entitled, trained by Vincent O'Brien and third in the Irish Derby, the unbeaten Broken Hearted, facile winner of the Extel Stakes at Goodwood and an impressive conqueror at Deauville of Saint Andrews and the subsequent

## Dunnes Stores St Bernard Phoenix Champion Stakes

Phoenix Park
1¼ miles
6 September 1987

| | | |
|---|---|---|
| 1 Triptych | A. Cruz | 5–4 fav. |
| 2 Entitled | D. Gillespie | 14–1 |
| 3 Cockney Lass | M. Kinane | 25–1 |

*Also ran:* Ascot Knight (4th), Risk Me, Motley, Sharp Noble, Broken Hearted, Fair Judgement, Invited Guest, Island Reef, Groom Dancer

12 ran

Winner owned by A. Clore, trained by P-L. Biancone

*Distances:* neck, 2½ lengths

*Tony Cruz pushes Triptych clear of Entitled.*

Arc winner Trempolino, and Risk Me, who had won the Grand Prix de Paris at Longchamp. In all twelve runners entered the stalls, but it was by no means the strongest field that Triptych had ever faced and she was a very warm favourite at 5–4, with Broken Hearted 6–1 and Risk Me and Ascot Knight (who had not been out since his defeat at York) on 13–2.

The race saw the typical Triptych, and a typical Tony Cruz performance on her. As the mare got older she became more convinced that she and she alone knew how a race should be run, and woe betide the jockey who tried to harry her. Cruz's handling of her was never less than in complete sympathy with her frame of mind, and now he held her up in the early stages and let her run her race in her own time. As the runners swung right-handed into the straight and faced up towards the stands, she decided that the moment had come to make her presence felt, and with cool confidence Cruz steered her over to the rails, from where she started to go past her rivals. Inside the final furlong there was only Entitled to beat, but Triptych could clearly pick him off at her ease, and just before the winning post Cruz encouraged her to lengthen her already raking stride. Head in the air as usual, she edged scornfully past her fully extended rival and at the winning post had beaten him by a neck.

The rest of 1987 saw Triptych racing in France (third in the Arc), Britain (a win in the Dubai Champion Stakes) and Japan; and in 1988 she was back again. Her final racecourse appearance came in the Breeders' Cup Turf at Churchill Downs, Kentucky, finishing fourth to Great Communicator.

It was in Kentucky, the state where she was bred, that Triptych met her tragically untimely end the following spring. In the early hours of 24 May 1989 she was with other mares in a paddock at Claiborne Farm, where she had been covered by the stallion Mr Prospector, when the nightwatchman made his rounds in his truck. The mares stampeded at the truck and Triptych seems to have crashed into the back of the vehicle. It was not until the paddock was being checked over after the incident that she was found, lying on the ground and badly injured. She died of severe haemorrhaging on the way to the veterinary clinic. Tony Cruz offered one of many tributes: 'She was a real character with her own special personality.'

# PEBBLES

*Breeders' Cup Turf*
*Aqueduct, 2 November 1985*

## Breeders' Cup Turf

Aqueduct
1½ miles
2 November 1985

| 1 Pebbles | P. Eddery | 11–5 fav. |
|---|---|---|
| 2 Strawberry Road | S. Cauthen | 19–5 |
| 3 Mourjane | R. Migliore | 51–1 |

*Also ran:* Danger's Hour (4th), Greinton, Teleprompter, Who's For Dinner, Baillamont, Theatrical, Bob Back, Persian Tiara, Sharannpour, Lashkari, Shernazar

14 ran

Winner owned by Sheikh Mohammed Al-Maktoum, trained by C. Brittain

*Distances:* neck, 1¼ lengths

❛ *Pebbles acts as a tonic to any race in which she competes* ❜

To the *New York Times*, Pebbles was 'the English filly who drinks a pint of stout every morning and went to post in the company of a British gelding she has a crush on'; in the 1985 Breeders' Cup Turf at Aqueduct she 'overcame a poor start and traffic problems to beat the boys by a neck' and provide Britain's first win in a Breeders' Cup event.

The four-year-old Pebbles who travelled to New York was already one of the toughest and most popular fillies of recent years. She had won two of her six races as a two-year-old and finished a neck second (at 33–1) to Desirable in the Cheveley Park Stakes at Newmarket, the most important race for two-year-old fillies run in Britain. As a three-year-old she won the Nell Gwyn Stakes at Newmarket before coasting home by three lengths in the One Thousand Guineas, after which she was sold by owner-breeder Captain Marcos Lemos to Sheikh Mohammed. In her first run in the Sheikh's colours she came second to Katies in the Coronation Stakes at Royal Ascot and in October was a strong-finishing second, beaten a neck, to Palace Music in the Champion Stakes. Kept in training as a four-year-old, Pebbles won the Trusthouse Forte Mile at Sandown Park, was second in the Prince of Wales's Stakes at Royal Ascot, and then became the first filly ever to win the Eclipse, beating subsequent Arc winner Rainbow Quest by two lengths. She was rested until October, when she beat the Derby winner Slip Anchor by three lengths in the Champion Stakes at Newmarket, showing brilliant acceleration to pull clear of a top-class field which also included Commanche Run and Helen Street.

Pebbles was an outstanding racehorse, but the Breeders' Cup bid was none the less a characteristically bold move on the part of trainer Clive Brittain, for the Turf race is over one and a half miles and she had never raced beyond ten furlongs. In her favour, though, was the configuration of the Aqueduct track: at a little over seven furlongs round it is very tight, and demands the pace to lic in a handy position, the balance to negotiate the turns, and the acceleration to dominate the race in the home straight. Pebbles had all three in abundance, and these would counter her doubtful stamina.

There were fourteen runners. Pebbles, whose owner had been required to stump up $240,000 to supplement her as a late entry, started 11–5 favourite, with Greinton (whose gallant run against Teleprompter in the Arlington Million two months earlier is described on pages 96–7) at 13–5. Next in the betting on 19–5 was Bob Back, who earlier in the season had sprung a surprise by beating Pebbles and Commanche Run at Royal Ascot, though Pebbles had got her revenge in the Eclipse; he had been trained in England by Michael Jarvis, but was now in the care of Angel Penna in the USA. Also on 19–5 was the six-year-old Strawberry Road, champion colt in Australia as a three-year-old and winner of several good races in France, where he was now based. Teleprompter himself was back to try to lift another mammoth American prize: but though he had run second to Shadeed in the Queen Elizabeth II Stakes at Ascot since his wonderful victory in Chicago, another English challenger, Shergar's half-brother Shernazar, was more strongly fancied, for he had beaten Slip Anchor at Kempton Park in September. French-trained Lashkari, owned like Shernazar by the Aga Khan, had won the inaugural running of the Turf in 1984 but had not seemed at his best in 1985. The European contingent was completed by Baillamont, trained by François Boutin, and Theatrical, trained in Ireland by Dermot Weld and second to Law Society in the Irish Derby.

Steve Cauthen had partnered Pebbles in her first three races of the season but Pat Eddery had ridden her with sublime confidence in the Champion Stakes when Cauthen was claimed for Slip Anchor, and it was Eddery who had the mount at Aqueduct. In the early stages he was content to keep her towards the rear of the field as Teleprompter – also attempting a mile and a half for the first time – took his accustomed role of front-runner. As in the Million, Teleprompter soon had the field at full pelt, and he tore down the back stretch and round the final bend. Pebbles had to snatch up briefly to avoid scrimmaging in front of her on the tight final bend, and for a second it looked as though she might be shut in. But as those boxing her in came away from the rails at the

ABOVE *Pebbles and Pat Eddery return to unsaddle, with trainer Clive Brittain (light raincoat) looking well satisfied.*

LEFT *Pebbles waltzes clear of Strawberry Road.*

entrance to the home stretch she found a good run up the inside, and when Tele-propmter ran out of stamina with just over a furlong to go Pat Eddery shot the favourite into the lead and made for the wire. Pebbles stretched out her neck and responded to Eddery's exhortations with the utmost gameness to go a length up. If there was any problem with her stamina this was where it would show – but as Steve Cauthen detached Strawberry Road from the pack she kept going strongly. Pebbles had not come this far to capitulate now, and at the wire she was a long-looking neck to the good. The 51–1 outsider Mourjane was third. Pebbles had broken the course re-cord and brought her owner $900,000 (£629,371 at the prevailing exchange rate),

the greatest amount ever won by an English-trained horse in a single race.

The Breeders' Cup Turf proved to be Peb-bles' last race. This enchanting white-faced chestnut could be excitable before her races – it was the Royal Hunt Cup winner Come On The Blues, her travelling companion and calming influence, on whom she had her crush – but was admirably genuine, and her home-stretch surge to bring British racing its first great triumph in the Breeders' Cup ensured that the affection in which she was held during her racing career would not fade. *Racehorses of 1985* encapsulated her appeal: 'Pebbles acts as a tonic to any race in which she competes.'

# PHAR LAP

*Agua Caliente Handicap*
*Tanforan, 20 March 1932*

*Phar Lap relaxes in his private sandbath during his preparation for the Agua Caliente race.*

The Agua Caliente Handicap at Tanforan, Mexico, in March 1932 saw the last racecourse appearance of a horse who was beyond dispute one of the greatest horses that ever raced – Phar Lap.

'The Red Terror', as Phar Lap was to become known, was a freak of breeding: his sire Night Raid failed to win at all in England before being sent to Australia, and his dam Entreaty was unplaced on her only start. He was foaled on the South Island of New Zealand, and his entry in the catalogue for the 1928 Trentham Yearling Sales took the eye of Sydney-based trainer Harry Telford, who persuaded owner David Davis to send in a bid for the horse. Davis agreed to go up to 200 guineas, and in the event secured the unseen yearling for a mere 160 guineas. Subsequent events were to make the horse a leading candidate for the greatest bloodstock bargain of all time, but when the new owner first saw his purchase he was horrified. On his arrival in Australia the unnamed chestnut colt was a tall, ungainly and unsightly animal with no hint of quality, and Davis so regretted his outlay, however modest, that the only way Telford could keep the horse in training was to make an arrangement with Davis whereby Telford himself took a three-year lease on the horse, taking two thirds of any prize money won in return for footing the training bill.

The colt was named Phar Lap, Sinhalese for 'lightning'. He was gelded and given time to mature a little before being asked to race, and he did not make his debut until 23 February 1929. He scored once as a two-year-old, in his final outing of five. As a three-year-old he was unplaced in his first four races then ran a good second in the Chelmsford Stakes at Randwick. In the Rosehill Gui-

neas a week later Phar Lap won easily, and then took the AJC Derby, the Craven Plate and the Victoria Derby. Despite the reservations of his trainer he next went for the Melbourne Cup: he started even-money favourite, but pulled his way to the front in a slowly run race against the wishes of his jockey and faded in the straight to finish third. This was but a temporary setback, for after a rest and a defeat on his return he proceeded to win his next nine races, completely outclassing his rivals at distances from nine furlongs to two and a quarter miles. His most spectacular success came in the AJC PLate, where he handed out a ten-length beating to his Melbourne Cup conqueror Nightmarch.

At four he lost only on the first and last outings (beaten narrowly on both occasions) of a sixteen-race campaign. He competed in handicaps and in weight-for-age races, and over distances from seven furlongs to two miles. On the morning of the Melbourne Stakes, which was to be Phar Lap's warm-up race for the Melbourne Cup three days later, he was shot at from the window of a car as he returned from exercise. The would-be assassins missed their prey, and Phar Lap, unperturbed by the incident,

*Phar Lap scorches in from Reveille Boy.*

## Agua Caliente Handicap

Tanforan
1¹/₄ miles
20 March 1932

| 1 | Phar Lap | W. Elliott | 6–4 fav. |
| 2 | Reveille Boy | R. Wholey | 72–10 |
| 3 | Scimitar | G. Smith | 282–10 |

*Also ran:* Joe Flores (4th), Marine, Good and Hot, Seth's Hope, Spanish Play, Dr Freeland, Bahamas, Cabezo

11 ran

Winner owned by D. J. Davis and H. R. Telford, trained by T. Woodcock

*Distances:* 2 lengths, 3 lengths

duly won the Stakes and then ran one of his most brilliant races to lift the Cup, for which he carried nine stone twelve pounds and started at 11–8 on, the shortest-priced favourite in the history of the race.

In February 1931 Telford bought a half-share in the horse shortly before his lease ran out, and henceforth Phar Lap was the joint property of Davis and Telford. By the time of his third Melbourne Cup in November he had already won eight races as a five-year-old and had become a national idol, but the handicapper had shovelled ten stone ten pounds on his back for the Cup, so it was no disgrace when he could finish only eighth. The winner White Nose carried three stone twelve pounds less than 'The Red Terror'.

The 1931 Melbourne Cup was Phar Lap's last race in Australia. The intention was to continue his career in the USA, and he was shipped to California, where, trained by Tommy Woodcock, his first target was the Agua Caliente Handicap, originally billed as the world's richest horse race and run just over the Mexican border in Tanforan, out of reach of California's restrictive betting legislation. Some 15,000 spectators – mostly from California – had come to see the world's greatest horse, who had top weight of nine stone three pounds in a field of eleven. His highest weighted opponent was the 1929 Preakness winner Dr Freeland with eight stone eight pounds, but the horse most fancied to give him a true test in his first race outside Australia was Spanish Play, who had won the New Orleans Handicap eight days before. Reveille Boy, at six the same age as Phar Lap but here in receipt of eleven pounds, had won the American Derby in 1930. Phar Lap started at 6–4, Spanish Play 3–1, Joe Flores and Cabezo were coupled on 13–2, and Reveille Boy was 72–10.

Phar Lap was ridden by Bill 'Urn' Elliott, who got the gelding smartly into his stride, but Phar Lap drifted right over to the outside rail, with the result that after a quarter of a mile of the ten-furlong race he was well adrift of the field. But having had his look at the outside Phar Lap returned to join the rest of the pack, and though he remained at the rear he was going very easily. With about half a mile to go Elliott decided that it was time to make a move, and in a matter of a few

strides Phar Lap had stormed up from last to first. Coming round the final bend he had opened up a substantial lead and seemed to be coasting home. Elliott began to take things easy and Reveille Boy, who had been in hot pursuit for some time, reduced the gap. He was a high-class horse and under strong driving came upsides, but the jockey was not bothered. One slap from his whip and Phar Lap cruised into the lead again, winning by two lengths in a course record time and hardly coming off the bridle.

Phar Lap was now poised to conquer further heights in America, but just over two weeks later he was dead, apparently as a result of having eaten grass or plants which had been sprayed with an insecticide. Rumours that he had been deliberately poisoned were generally discredited, but the exact cause of his death was never established.

What was established beyond doubt was that Phar Lap, winner of thirty-seven of his fifty-one races, was one of the finest race-horses ever. Much of his extraordinary combination of speed and stamina can be attributed to his physique. Over 17 hands high, he had a girth which measured seventy-nine inches (Secretariat's girth was thought to be remarkably large at seventy-six inches) and housed a heart which after his death tipped the scales at fourteen and a half pounds: the average for a Thoroughbred is around ten pounds. He was tough, he was genuine, he was durable, he was versatile. Reassuringly, he was also good-natured: he loved having his tongue pulled.

Half a century after his death he was paid the unusual tribute of becoming the subject of a feature film. At the very end of the movie *Phar Lap* a newspaper reporter in Australia seeks out trainer Harry Telford, who has just received news of the horse's tragic end. 'Why is it, do you think, that there's been this incredible reaction to Phar Lap's death?' asks the reporter: 'After all, he was just a horse.' 'He wasn't just a horse,' snaps Telford: 'He was the best.'

# ARKLE

*❛ It was a spectacle which I shall never forget ❜*

An exhibition round: Arkle leads Mill House on the first circuit.

If the 1964 Cheltenham Gold Cup (see pages 26–8) was Arkle's coronation, the Gallaher Gold Cup at Sandown Park in November 1965 produced his greatest individual performance, an astonishing burst of acceleration which demolished any lingering doubts about his exceptional quality.

In the year and a half which had elapsed since the famous showdown between Arkle and Mill House at Cheltenham their fortunes had contrasted starkly. Arkle had won six races (including the Irish Grand National, the Hennessy Gold Cup, a second Chelten-

ham Gold Cup and the Whitbread Gold Cup) and been narrowly beaten once, when conceding large amounts of weight to top-class horses Flying Wild and Buona Notte in the Massey-Ferguson Handicap Chase at Cheltenham. Mill House had won three of his seven races but seemed to be in decline as his rival rose to yet greater heights.

The gulf which had opened up between them was apparent from the weights for the Gallaher Gold Cup: Arkle was set to carry twelve stone seven pounds, Mill House eleven stone five pounds, a difference of sixteen pounds. Among their rivals were several good chasers – Rondetto, The Rip and John O'Groats – but the big two dominated the betting, Arkle starting 9–4 on with Mill House at 7–2. There was a feeling that Mill House might *just* be coming out of the doldrums: he had won his last race, beating his solitary rival at Sandown Park for the princely sum of £426, and appeared to be coming back to his old self. The memory was still fresh of the time when he was considered a world-beater, and in receipt of so much weight from Arkle he could certainly be given a realistic chance.

Thus an air of tremendous expectation hung in the autumn air as the runners filed out of the paddock down to the course, Arkle ridden as usual by Pat Taaffe and Mill House on this occasion by David Nicholson, as his usual partner Willie Robinson was injured. The feeling that something special was about to happen spilled over into an exhibition of appreciation then unparalleled on an English racecourse: the crowd applauded the rivals as they made their way on to the track and burst into cheering as they reached it.

Nor did the cheering cease when the runners got down to business and the three-mile race commenced, for at almost every fence Arkle and Mill House produced leaps which drew from the spectators whoops of appreciation. As they turned into the straight on the first circuit Mill House, jumping like a buck, had the lead, with Arkle pulling hard in his wake and taking his fences superbly. The cheers melted into gasps of admiration and roars of approval from the stands as, in turn, this famous pair of chasers made some of the most prodigious leaps

## Gallaher Gold Cup

Sandown Park
3 miles 118 yards
6 November 1965

| 1 Arkle | P. Taaffe | 4–9 fav. |
| 2 Rondetto | J. King | 9–1 |
| 3 Mill House | D. Nicholson | 7–2 |

*Also ran:* The Rip (4th), Lira, Candy, John O' Groats

7 ran

Winner owned by Anne, Duchess of Westminster, trained by T. W. Dreaper

*Distances:* 20 lengths, 4 lengths

ever seen on an English racecourse,' wrote Len Thomas in the *Sporting Life*: 'It was a spectacle which I shall never forget.'

The cheering swelled as they passed the stands, and as they turned down the hill for the second circuit Taaffe could no longer restrain Arkle, who took up the running. Down the far side the two cleared the first three fences with speed and accuracy, and at the water jump Mill House, swinging along just like the 'Big Horse' of old, regained the lead. Less than a mile to go as they pinged over the three obstacles set close together at the far end of the back straight, and Mill House was all of three lengths ahead: as they stretched out round the long sweeping turn towards the Pond Fence, the third from home, it really seemed as if he was at last going to take his revenge on Arkle.

What happened next will never be forgotten by anyone who witnessed it: in an instant Arkle swept contemptuously past Mill House to open up an unassailable lead. He had caught up with and passed his rival in a matter of a few strides in a quite extraordinary spurt of acceleration for a steeple-chaser carrying twelve and a half stone at the end of a three-mile chase, and for the big horse it was simply too much: Mill House weakened rapidly and by the time Arkle had strode home to a rapturous reception Mill House had been passed by Rondetto. Arkle won by twenty lengths, with Mill House four lengths back in third. It then transpired that Arkle, under no pressure, had beaten the course record for the distance by no less than eleven seconds.

Arkle and Mill House did not meet again. Arkle continued to prove himself a chaser of extraordinary ability – in effect, a freak – before untimely retirement was forced on him after he broke a bone in his foot in the 1966 King George VI Chase at Kempton Park, while Mill House had his own moment of Sandown Park glory when winning the Whitbread Gold Cup in a desperate finish in 1967. That day emotion ran high as the big horse, so long the underdog, at last had his day again. But for sheer quality of performance, nothing in modern steeplechasing history matches Arkle's acceleration on that final bend in the Gallaher Gold Cup.

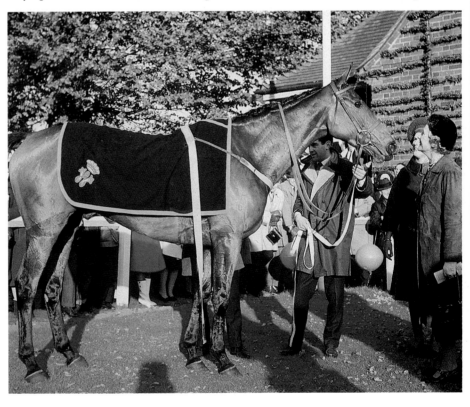

*Arkle after the race with owner Anne, Duchess of Westminster (green coat) and trainer's wife Betty Dreaper.*

# JOHN HENRY

*Arlington Million*
*Arlington Park, 30 August 1981*

❛ *This is the toughest little dude I've ever seen* ❜

John Henry was retired in July 1985 after a racing career over eight seasons which made him one of the most popular horses ever to run in the USA. Horse of the Year in 1981 and 1984, his earnings were $6,597,947 from eighty-three starts, of which he won thirty-nine. None of his victories was more characteristic of his indomitable will to win than his first success in the Arlington Million.

Foaled in 1975 and humbly bred, John Henry changed hands three times before reaching Dot and Sam Rubin's Dotsam Stables (Sam Rubin bought the horse unseen over the phone, and did not at the time know that his new purchase was a gelding). John Henry won his first race for his new owner and ten days later took a $35,000 claiming race on grass at Belmont Park by fourteen lengths. Gelding or not, John Henry was quite a horse, and by the end of his first season with Rubin he had won six races, including five on grass (of which two were Stakes races).

In the spring of 1979 he moved from trainer Bobby Donato to V. J. ('Lefty') Nickerson in New York, with whom he continued to show his preference for racing on grass rather than on dirt. But opportunities for races on grass on the East coast were limited, so he was flown out to California to join Ron McAnally, in whose charge he won a division of the $40,000 Henry P. Russell Handicap. By the end of May 1980 – in

which year he first raced on 1 January – he had won six out of six in California and Florida. Then it was back to Nickerson in the East for a campaign which included a second in the Jockey Club Gold Cup and a third in the Turf Classic. Then California again, for a brave victory in the Oak Tree International. That year he won an Eclipse Award as champion grass horse, though he was rated eight pounds below Spectacular Bid, the Horse Of The Year. In 1981 John Henry was a six-year-old. He won his first four races in California but after a defeat was off to Nickerson again: do horses qualify for Frequent Flyer privileges? He won the Sword Dancer Stakes in July, with 50-year-old Bill Shoemaker replacing his regular jockey Laffit Pincay. After a short rest in California, John Henry was flown to Chicago for the inaugural Arlington Million.

The field of twelve was truly international, with runners from England, Ireland, France and Canada as well as the USA. Lester Piggott rode Madam Gay, winner of the Prix de Diane at Chantilly (the French Oaks) and second to Shergar in the King George VI and Queen Elizabeth Diamond Stakes at Ascot the month before the Million. Steve Cauthen rode another English challenger in Fingal's Cave, a short head behind Madam Gay at Ascot. The French horse Argument had won the Prix Ganay at Longchamp earlier in the season. John Henry, coupled for betting purposes with his stable-mate Super Moment, was 11–10 favourite.

It was not only the top-class international field which made John Henry's task a stiff one, for days of heavy rain – which persisted during the race – had made the going very soft, conditions which the gelding did not like. And John Henry was drawn on the outside in the starting gate at number 12. From this position he could not expect to be prominent going to the first bend, the club-house turn, and Shoemaker held him back in about eighth place, some four horses out from the rails, as the runners came past the stands. Once in the back stretch the jockey manoeuvred John Henry across to the rails, but the horse was ill at ease on the soggy ground and appeared to be out of contention. Then he started to pick off his rivals, but time was slipping by and up in front outsider

*John Henry (near side) comes to collar The Bart.*

## Arlington Million

Arlington Park
1¾ miles
30 August 1981

| | | |
|---|---|---|
| 1 John Henry | W. Shoemaker | 11–10 fav. |
| 2 The Bart | E. Delahoussaye | 407–10 |
| 3 Madam Gay | L. Piggott | 123–10 |

*Also ran:* Key To Content (4th), Match Of The Hatch, Argument, Mrs Penny, Rossi Gold, Super Moment, Kilijaro, Fingal's Cave, P'Tite Tete

12 ran

Winner owned by Dotsam Stables, trained by R. McAnally

*Distances:* nose, 2½ lengths

The Bart had taken up the running from the pacemaking Key To Content. The Bart, who had been trained in Ireland before being moved to California, had gone clear as the runners came into the home stretch, and Lester Piggott was trying to bring Madam Gay along the rails. As the filly made her move John Henry started to pick up ground on the outside; the Bart still looked the winner, but John Henry was beginning to catch him, and Shoemaker now produced one of the greatest finishes of his extraordinary career. Having persuaded the gelding to run on, he now crouched right into the horse, keeping him completely balanced on ground which he hated and doing nothing to disrupt his rhythm. Coaxing, pushing, imploring, the most successful jockey in the history of racing now had one of the toughest horses ever to race desperate to win, and John Henry started to make for the leader as if his life depended on it. With a hundred yards to go it still seemed that The Bart could not be caught, but John Henry had built up such momentum with his long stretch run up the outside that he might just do it. Up came Shoemaker's whip, and the horse seemed to lunge at his rival. John Henry collared The Bart right on the line, and it was impossible to say which had won.

The announcer for NBC thought he knew, and called The Bart the winner, but when the photograph was developed it showed that John Henry had got up by a nose.

Then came the tributes. 'He had the worst post position and this soft turf wasn't his type of racetrack,' said trainer Ron McAnally, 'but I never saw him run a better race.' Shoemaker was more direct: 'This is the toughest little dude I've ever seen.' John Henry ran twice more in the Arlington Million. In 1983 he was second to Tolomeo (beaten a neck) and in 1984, at the age of nine, he raised the roof of Arlington Park by beating Royal Heroine. He ran many other great races, including a neck victory over the French mare All Along in the 1984 Turf Classic at Aqueduct; but for the quintessential John Henry and the quintessential Bill Shoemaker, the 1981 Million is the race.

ABOVE *John Henry and Bill Shoemaker know they've been in a race.*

RIGHT *John Henry in retirement with trainer Ron McAnally.*

ABOVE *Sea Bird II swoops home from Reliance.*

OPPOSITE *Owner Jean Ternynck leads in Sea Bird II and Pat Glennon.*

The victory of Sea Bird II in the 1965 Prix de l'Arc de Triomphe was a performance of such merit that it will for ever stand as a benchmark of excellence in Thoroughbred racing. For not only did he win Europe's most important race with consummate ease, in so doing he beat one of the best international fields ever assembled.

Though unpromisingly bred (his dam Sicalade had been sold as butchers' meat for the equivalent of £100 before he ever ran), Sea Bird was clearly an outstanding three-year-old, having won the Prix Greffulhe and the Prix Lupin on the way to possibly the most facile Derby victory ever seen: at Epsom he won hard held from subsequent Irish Derby hero Meadow Court, and followed his triumph with a similarly easy win in the Grand Prix de Saint-Cloud. But he

faced formidable opposition in the Arc. The three-year-old Reliance was unbeaten in five races, including the Prix du Jockey-Club (the French Derby), the Grand Prix de Paris and the Prix Royal-Oak (the French St Leger). The filly Blabla had won the Prix de Diane (the French Oaks). From Ireland came three runners, including Meadow Court, who since his Irish Derby had won Britain's most important all-age race, the King George VI and Queen Elizabeth Stakes at Ascot. England was represented by the four-year-olds Soderini, winner of the John Porter Stakes and the Hardwicke Stakes, and Oncidium, victor in the Coronation Cup. Marco Visconti had travelled from Italy, Anilin was the first ever Russian-trained runner in the Arc, and from the USA came the crack three-year-old Tom Rolfe: an unlucky third

**Prix de l'Arc de Triomphe**

Longchamp
2400 metres
3 October 1965

| 1 | Sea Bird II | T. P. Glennon | 6–5 fav. |
| 2 | Reliance | Y. Saint-Martin | 9–2 |
| 3 | Diatome | J. Deforge | 15–2 |

*Also ran:* Free Ride (4th), Anilin, Tom Rolfe, Demi Deuil, Carvin, Meadow Court, Marco Visconti, Timmy Lad, Emerald, Ragazzo, Francilius, Sigebert, Ardaban, Soderini, Oncidium, Khalife, Blabla

20 ran

Winner owned by J. Ternynck, trained by E. Pollet

*Distances:* 6 lengths, 5 lengths

in the Kentucky Derby, winner of the Preakness and narrowly beaten in the Belmont, then winner of the American Derby at Arlington Park, the Arc was his thirteenth race of the season. In all, twenty runners went to post.

A notoriously highly-strung horse, Sea Bird sweated freely during the preliminaries, but this did not prevent his starting a warm favourite at 6–5. With the early pace being set by Marco Visconti, the Australian jockey Pat Glennon kept the Derby winner in a group just behind the leaders with Tom Rolfe (Bill Shoemaker), Meadow Court (Lester Piggott) and Reliance (Yves Saint-Martin). Down the hill towards the straight Marco Visconti gave way to Anilin, but Sea

Bird was still cantering, and he swept past the Russian challenger with Reliance in hot pursuit. As two brilliant French three-year-olds detached themselves from the rest of the field the scene was set for a stirring head-to-head struggle, but when Glennon gave Sea Bird his head the horse shot away from his rival with an electrifying burst of acceleration which quickly took him several lengths clear, despite his veering from the far rail towards the middle of the course.

Sea Bird's official winning margin over Reliance was six lengths; that another high-class French three-year-old, Diatome, was a further five lengths back in third is more evidence of the magnitude of the winner's performance. Free Ride was fourth, Anilin fifth, Tom Rolfe sixth, Demi Deuil seventh, Carvin eighth and Meadow Court ninth.

In the excited aftermath of the race, Pat Glennon described his mount as 'by far the best horse I have ever seen – let alone ridden' and Yves Saint-Martin pronounced him '*un crack prodigieux*', while Quintin Gilbey, *doyen* of British racing journalists, proclaimed Sea Bird's Arc 'the greatest performance by any horse in my time'. As eloquent as the human tributes were the subsequent records of the horses whom he so comprehensively thrashed at Longchamp: Anilin went on to win the Grosser Preis von Europa, Germany's top race; Diatome and Carvin ran first and second in the Washington International; and Demi Deuil sauntered home in the Premio Roma. Reliance did not run again.

Nor did Sea Bird. Never extended as a three-year-old, it is impossible to know just how good he was, though for most racing enthusiasts he remains the best horse to have run in Europe since the Second World War. He commenced his stud career in the USA before returning to France, and among his offspring were Allez France, one of the greatest racemares ever and herself winner of the Arc in 1974, and the dual Champion Hurdler Sea Pigeon.

But it is the sight of Sea Bird II striding contemptuously away from a top international field in the Paris sunshine in October 1965 which lingers in racing's collective memory. That afternoon he was everything a racehorse should be.

# TULLOCH

*Caulfield Cup*
*Caulfield, 19 October 1957*

The Caulfield Cup is a twelve-furlong handicap which usually attracts some of the best weight-for-age horses in Australia and New Zealand (and exerts a considerable influence on prognostications for Australia's greatest race, the Melbourne Cup run at Flemington, Melbourne's other major course, a couple of weeks later). In 1957 it saw a performance by Tulloch which bolstered the claim that this three-year-old colt was at that time the best horse in the world.

Tulloch, who had been sold as a yearling for a mere 750 guineas, first ran at Randwick in September 1956 and by the end of the 1956–7 term had progressed into one of the two top juveniles in Australia, with seven wins to his credit including the AJC Sires' Produce Stakes, the VRC Sires' Produce Stakes, and the QTC Sires' Produce Stakes – the three major two-year-old events of the season. In the AJC Sires' Produce Stakes he had beaten the brilliantly speedy Todman over seven furlongs, but Todman took his revenge over a furlong less four days later in the Champagne Stakes, and by the end of the season they were rated equals.

The following season it became apparent that Todman's forte was shorter distances, while Tulloch got better as he tackled longer trips. He opened his three-year-old account with a win in the AJC Warwick Stakes and, in the absence of the injured Todman, took the ten-furlong Rosehill Guineas from Prince Darius, whom he then beat by six lengths in record time in the AJC Derby over a mile and a half at Randwick. It was now reasonable to contemplate the Caulfield Cup–Melbourne Cup double. This was a mouth-watering notion, for by October 1957 Tulloch had shown himself one of the very best horses ever to have raced in Australia. The double had been pulled off as recently as 1954 by Rising Fast, but he had been a five-year-old, and Tulloch's owner Mr Haley did not hide his reluctance to run a three-year-old in the two-mile Melbourne Cup.

By this time Tulloch was still only 15.2 hands high, but he had grown into a handsome horse with a huge stride for one so small, and many thought him perfectly capable of lugging to victory the eight stone four pounds he had been allotted for the

Melbourne Cup – five pounds more than the record weight carried by a winning three-year-old. First, though, there was the Caulfield Cup, for which Tulloch warmed up with an easy success in the Caulfield Guineas a week before the big race.

Tulloch carried seven stone eight pounds in the Caulfield, nearly two stone less than the five-year-old Sailor's Guide, who had won the Victoria Derby in 1955 and now had to hump top weight. Destined to take the Washington International a year later on the disqualification of Tudor Era, Sailor's Guide had carried nine stone twelve pounds into second place behind Syntax in the Turnbull Stakes at Flemington earlier in the month and had won the Craiglee Stakes on that course. He was a high-class horse, but for the Cup he started at 7–1. Top Fred had won on eight of the nine starts of his career, and Mac's Amber came to the race fresh from a victory under nine stone four pounds in a big handicap at Caulfield a week earlier: he carried the same weight in the Cup.

Tulloch was ridden by Neville Sellwood – who had won the race twice before – as his regular jockey George Moore could not do the weight, and was the first odds-on favourite in the history of the race at 6–4 on in a field of seventeen. This cramped price was understandable, for his obvious claims on form were complemented by the tremendous confidence shown by his connections beforehand. When on the day before the race worries were aired about Tulloch's draw – on the outside of the seventeen – trainer Tommy Smith breezily assured the press, 'He has to start from somewhere, and he will win it just the same.'

There was a run of a quarter of a mile to the first bend, so Sellwood had plenty of time to get Tulloch settled in behind from his outside draw. He managed this without undue difficulty, but much of the left-handed Caulfield circuit is on the turn, and in the middle of the race his supporters had some anxious moments. Tulloch appeared to be badly hemmed in by the big field and as Mac's Amber led into the short straight a sensational defeat was on the cards. With just three hundred yards to go Sellwood extricated Tulloch and asked him to go after Mac's Amber, on whom Bill Williamson was

## Caulfield Cup

Caulfield
2400 metres
19 October 1957

| | | |
|---|---|---|
| 1 Tulloch | N. Sellwood | 4–6 fav. |
| 2 Mac's Amber | W. Williamson | 16–1 |
| 3 Sailor's Guide | R. Hutchinson | 7–1 |

*Also ran:* Lord Gavin (4th), Nether Gold, Sandara, Flash Gem, Tudor Hill, Shadow Play, Gallant Lee, Royal Somme, Top Fred, Sunium, Sir William, White Hills, Zariba, Sandarine

17 ran

Winner owned by E. A. Haley, trained by T. J. Smith

*Distances:* 2 lengths, 1 length

making for home. The response was galvanic. In the words of VRC handicapper Charles Davis, Tulloch 'smothered them'. His gigantic stride got to work as soon as he was straightened up for the winning post, and with less than a furlong to go he swept past the leader to take the race by two lengths. Sailor's Guide was third.

Tulloch's time of 2 minutes 26.9 seconds beat the course record by nearly a second. The issue was settled with one telling burst of speed at the right time, and that was that. Trainer Tommy Smith stressed how little the effort had taken out of his charge: 'Sellwood said he coasted over the last bit. Twenty minutes after winning the Cup he would not have blown out a candle.'

In the immediate aftermath of the race

intense speculation revolved around whether Tulloch would take his chance in the Melbourne Cup. The prospects of his taking part at Flemington were front-page news, but despite Tommy Smith's enthusiasm for having a go the wishes of owner Haley prevailed, and he missed the race. He was by no means finished for the season, though, going on to win the Victoria Derby (beating Prince Darius by eight lengths at 10–1 on), the C. B. Fisher Plate (beating Sailor's Guide) and the Queensland Derby.

In all, Tulloch won thirty-six of his fifty-three races, and only once finished out of the first three. 'Tulloch is a freak,' said Tommy Smith: 'The secret of his greatness is that he is a stayer who can go like a sprinter in the big races.'

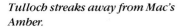

*Tulloch streaks away from Mac's Amber.*

# KELSO

*◖ It will be a long time before you see another like him ◗*

For half a decade one horse towered over all others in American racing: Kelso. This dark brown gelding was Horse Of The Year five times in a row, from 1960 to 1964. He landed the Jockey Club Gold Cup in each of those five years and the Woodward Stakes three times. In all he won thirty-nine of his sixty-three starts. In November 1964, when a seven-year-old, he won the Washington International at the fourth attempt.

Bred by Mrs Allaire duPont, owner of Woodstock Farm in Maryland, and foaled in 1957 at Claiborne Farm in Kentucky, where she then kept her mares, Kelso was gelded as a two-year-old. He did not run until the September of that year, making a winning debut in a six-furlong maiden race and finishing second in his other two races. He was trained as a two-year-old by John Lee but now came under the charge of Carl Hanford, with whom he was to remain for the rest of his career. He did not begin his three-year-old campaign until late June, when he won by ten lengths at Monmouth Park and followed up with a twelve-length victory at Aqueduct. But these were both minor events, and when Kelso took on better oppo-

sition in the Arlington Classic he finished only eighth behind T.V. Lark. Back on the East Coast, he won three good races before scoring impressively in the Lawrence Realisation over one mile five furlongs, equalling Man O' War's track record in the same race in 1920. Then it was back to Illinois to win the Hawthorne Gold Cup before his first victory in the Jockey Club Gold Cup, at that time run over two miles. Here he was opposed by the great Bald Eagle, winner of the Washington International in 1959 and shortly to win it again: in soft going Kelso knocked nearly three seconds off the American record for the distance, with Bald Eagle back in third. Kelso was now a star, and became Horse of the Year for the first time.

In 1961 he won the 'Handicap Triple Crown' at Aqueduct – the Metropolitan, the Suburban and the Brooklyn – and was Horse of the Year again; but his first run in the Washington International had ended in defeat. At odds of 5–2 on he was beaten three quarters of a length by T.V. Lark and, worse, suffered an injury which kept him off the track for over six months. In 1962 he won six races, and in 1963 nine, but again found one horse too good in the

*Kelso wins the Washington International at last.*

International – this time the American runner Mongo.

So Kelso came to Laurel Park in November 1964 with a frustrating record to improve upon: three runs, three times runner-up. It seemed that only Gun Bow, one of the best handicap horses for many years, offered a serious challenge, and he was a familiar rival. Kelso had finished in front of Gun Bow when they were both beaten by Mongo in the Monmouth Stakes; Gun Bow had beaten Kelso in the Brooklyn Handicap, for which Mrs duPont's gelding had taken his revenge in the Aqueduct Stakes. They next met in the Woodward, and after a rousing struggle up the home stretch Kelso was beaten by inches. He then won the Jockey Club Gold Cup from Roman Brother and the Belmont Stakes winner Quadrangle to become the leading money-earner in world racing.

Despite his age Kelso was clearly in fine fettle, and in this year's Washington International he went off favourite, marginally preferred to Gun Bow. The other six runners advertised the international nature of the race: they came from France (Belle Sicambre, winner of the Prix de Diane and ridden by Lester Piggott), Ireland (Biscayne, winner of the Irish St Leger), Russia (Anilin, winner of the Soviet Derby and the most outstanding Russian colt for some time), Italy (Veronese), Japan (Ryu Forel) and Venezuela (Primordial).

After Biscayne had showed in the lead for a moment as the tapes went up Walter Blum pushed Gun Bow to the front, with Milo Valenzuela on Kelso going in immediate pursuit and the foreign visitors unable to get to the home team. Coming past the stands Gun Bow's blinkers and large sheepskin noseband showed in front, well clear of Kelso, with Belle Sicambre heading the posse of visitors, but already the International was becoming the two-horse race which the betting had predicted. Gun Bow veered around the bend and headed off down the back stretch, but Kelso still had him in his sights, and as they approached the halfway point Valenzuela asked him to close the gap. Gun Bow was an immensely speedy horse, in his element on the firm going and not inclined to give up the fight, but Kelso had caught up by the time a mile had been run, and as they

came round the final bend he edged into the lead. Belle Sicambre was five lengths behind the American pair and Ryu Forel three lengths further back, but as the two leaders raced neck and neck into the home stretch the distance between themselves and their rivals widened. With two furlongs to go Gun Bow still had the rail but Kelso was beginning to assert himself and go for the Washington International victory he so richly deserved. Gun Bow faltered and rolled out, brushing Kelso, but in a flash 'King Kelly' was away. As he went into the lead he moved over to the inside and seemed to cut in on Gun Bow. Valenzuela straightened him out and pushed him to the wire with hands and heels. Such was Kelso's acceleration that he had four and a half lengths to spare over Gun Bow at the line, with Anilin running on take third a further nine lengths back. Biscayne was fourth and Belle Sicambre fifth, earning $5000 for her effort – 'We've picked up enough money for breakfast,' Lester Piggott laconically told the press.

Kelso had clocked a time of 2 minutes 23.8 seconds, then the fastest twelve furlongs ever run in America, but Walter Blum objected to the winner on the grounds that Kelso had cut in on Gun Bow at the entrance to the straight. It took almost half an hour for the officials to reach their verdict: to the relief of the 38,000-strong crowd the objection was overruled.

Kelso ran six times as an eight-year-old, winning the Whitney Stakes and two other races, and once as a nine-year-old. He was then retired to Mrs duPont's Woodstock Farm near Chesapeake City, from where his owner regularly hunted him with the local hounds. One of the most loved horses ever to run in America, his fame far outlasted his racing career and kept him in great demand for public appearances. He appeared at Belmont Park in 1983 the day before he died of colic at the age of twenty-six.

A plaque on the wall outside his box at Woodstock Farm read, 'The most durable horse in racing history'. And Walter Blum, whose ride on Gun Bow was unable to prevent Kelso winning the Washington International at last, paid this tribute just after the race: 'Kelso is a great horse. It will be a long time before you see another like him.'

## Washington DC International

Laurel Park
1½ miles
11 November 1964

| 1 | Kelso | I. Valenzuela | 6–5 fav. |
| 2 | Gun Bow | W. Blum | 6–4 |
| 3 | Anilin | N. Nasibov | 172–10 |

*Also ran:* Biscayne (4th), Belle Sicambre, Primordial, Veronese, Ryu Forel

8 ran

Winner owned by Bohemia Stable, trained by C. H. Hanford

*Distances:* 4½ lengths, 9 lengths

# RIBOT

*Prix de l'Arc de Triomphe*
*Longchamp, 7 October 1956*

◀ *Whoosh!* ▶

*Ribot effortlessly wins his second Arc.*

Ribot, the finest racehorse to have come out of Italy, was unbeaten in sixteen races. He was bred by Federico Tesio, who had founded his stud on the shores of Lake Maggiore and built up his breeding operation into one of the most successful in bloodstock history: apart from Ribot and the almost equally brilliant Nearco (also unbeaten), Tesio bred several horses of the highest class, including Tenerani – Ribot's sire.

The smallest of Tesio's 1952 foals, Ribot was given the nickname *il piccolo* – the little one – but it was soon apparent to Tesio that in Ribot he had bred a horse who would prove his assertion that Tenerani could sire a champion. Sadly the breeder did not live to see his dream fulfilled: he died at the age of eighty-five in May 1954 just over two months before Ribot, by then in training with Ugo Penco, ran his first race.

That debut outing came at Milan in July 1954, where Ribot, racing in the colours of Tesio's long-time partner Marchese Mario

Incisa della Rochetta, won by a length. He then took the Criterium Nazionale and the Gran Criterium, Italy's most important two-year-old race. He had not been entered for the Italian Classics, but won the semi-Classic Premio Emanuele Filiberto by ten lengths and three other races before making his first entrance on the international stage in the 1955 Prix de l'Arc de Triomphe. Starting at almost 9–1, he won by three lengths in the hands of veteran jockey Enrico Camici, who rode him throughout his career. Ribot was clearly going from strength to strength, and before he finished for the season returned to Italy for the Gran Premio del Jockey Club at Milan, putting fifteen lengths between himself and his nearest rival, the French horse Norman, who had won the race in the previous two seasons.

Nine races, nine wins; but the best of Ribot was to come, and an ambitious four-year-old career was mapped out. After three wins in minor events he won the Gran Premio di Milano over one mile seven furlongs

Longchamp
2400 metres
7 October 1956

| 1 | Ribot | E. Camici | 6–10 fav. |
| 2 | Talgo | E. Mercer | 100–1 |
| 3 | Tanerko | J. Doyasbere | 8–1 |

*Also ran:* Career Boy (4th), Master Boing, Oroso, Fric, Burgos, Fisherman, Arabian, Cobetto, Zarathustra, Norfolk, Flying Flag, Saint Raphael, Ambiax, Tenareze, Vattel, Sicarelle, Apollonia

20 ran

Winner owned by Marchese Incisa della Rocchetta, trained by V. U. Penco

*Distances:* 6 lengths, 2 lengths

by eight lengths from Tissot. He then went to England for the King George VI and Queen Elizabeth Stakes at Ascot. Ribot started at 5–2 on but made heavy weather of it on the rain-saturated ground, and not until he encountered better going in the straight did his superb action make its presence felt. He won by five lengths, and it is indicative of the regard in which he was held in European racing by then that this was held to be his least impressive performance. He then won the Premio del Piazzale by eight lengths to make his career record fifteen out of fifteen. The undersized foal had become a giant of the Turf.

Nineteen horses stood between Ribot and a second Arc on the first Sunday in October, and the field that day was one of the strongest ever assembled. Fisherman had won the Washington International in 1954, and he was in the Arc to act as pacemaker for Career Boy, who had been runner-up in the Belmont Stakes. There were two winners of the Irish Derby – Zarathustra (1954) and Talgo (1956). Sicarelle had won the Oaks at Epsom earlier in the season, and Apollonia the French equivalent and the Poule d'Essai des Pouliches. Arabian had won the Prix Royal-Oak, Tanerko the Prix Lupin, Vattel the Grand Prix de Paris, and Burgos and Oroso had dead-heated in the Grand Prix de Saint-Cloud.

Despite this glittering array of talent from several countries and several generations, the other runners were no more than support acts for Ribot on what would be his final appearance in a race. He started at odds on, with Apollonia and Tanerko second and third favourites. That Talgo, who had won the Irish Derby earlier in the year, should start at 100–1 simply illustrates the class of the field, and what Ribot did to that field simply illustrates his greatness.

On going made heavy by a barrage of rain throughout the week before the race, Fisherman performed his pacemaking role well, pushing straight to the front and opening up a substantial lead. Ribot always disliked being held back too far off the pace, and in the early stages Camici kept the Italian superhorse handy in third position as the French four-year-old Norfolk moved up at halfway to take on Fisherman. Apollonia was

fourth. As the runners came down the hill towards the straight Fisherman still had a long lead and Norfolk could not get near him, but Camici was not rattled: he knew that under him he had a horse who had always dominated his rivals, and it was just a matter of time before Ribot went on to win his race. With more than a quarter of a mile to go Fisherman was running out of steam and Ribot was cruising, though behind him Tanerko and the outsider Talgo were in hot pursuit, and Eddie Arcaro on Career Boy was quite happy: 'I was going along there pretty good, fast enough to win it, I thought, when all of a sudden – whoosh! A horse took off from me so fast I couldn't recognize him.'

Whoosh indeed! Camici needed no recourse to the whip. He simply allowed Ribot a fraction more rein, and the reply from his horse was instant and conclusive. Ribot shot away from the finest international field of the age as if they were selling platers. This was his last race, and no time for restraint, so once Camici had brought Ribot's mighty engine to its full power he let the great horse stride out for the line in glorious isolation.

The official verdict was that Ribot won by six lengths, but in truth it was more like ten. Talgo was second, Tanerko third, and Career Boy fourth.

It was probably the most stunning individual performance seen in European racing since the war, and the future achievements of Ribot's opponents that day paid further tribute to the merit of his victory: the French horse Master Boing, fifth at Longchamp, won the Washington International the following month, Oroso won the Arc in 1957, and Zarathustra the Ascot Gold Cup that year.

Meanwhile Ribot himself had retired. He had run sixteen times and had hardly been extended, let alone beaten. He had won in three different countries and under very different conditions. He became a highly successful sire. At the Capanelle in Rome, in the second of two exhibition gallops staged for him after his 1956 Arc victory, he strode home well clear of his stable-companion Magistris and then, in a final flourish, dumped his constant partner Enrico Camici on the ground.

# TELEPROMPTER

*Arlington Million*
*Arlington Park, 25 August 1985*

❦ *Welcome Home Teleprompter – One in a Million* ❧

*Teleprompter sticks his tongue out...*

On 31 July 1985, less than a month before the fifth running of the Arlington Million, fire destroyed the 58-year-old grandstand at Arlington Park. But the racecourse authorities were determined that the event should go ahead, and by the time of the race the wreckage had been cleared away and temporary stands and a tented village erected; these Herculean efforts were rewarded when a crowd of over 35,000 turned up. This was the Miracle Million.

There was one disappointment, however. John Henry, who had won the first Million in 1981 (see pages 86–7), run second to Tolomeo in 1983 and won again in 1984, was missing: a tendon injury had sent him into retirement the previous month. But even as America's most famous gelding hung up his racing plates, Britain's best-loved Flat-race gelding was being prepared for his moment of international glory.

Teleprompter was a five-year-old, trained by Bill Watts at Richmond in Yorkshire. Gelded after his only outing as a two-year-old, this tall, strapping bay horse had become a familiar sight in the top races at distances around a mile. As a three-year-old he had won the Britannia Stakes at Royal Ascot and been beaten a head in the Cambridgeshire. As a four-year-old he was a close second under nine stone eleven pounds in the Royal Hunt Cup at Royal Ascot – his handsome head now encased in that large black pair of blinkers to help him concentrate, though he was always a thoroughly genuine horse – and then successfully made the transition to Pattern-race company when winning the Pacemaker International Stakes at Phoenix Park, the Tara Sires Desmond Stakes at The Curragh, the Prix Quincey at Deauville and the Queen Elizabeth II Stakes at Ascot, where he beat the Irish One Thousand Guineas winner Katies by a neck in a thrilling finish, rallying to regain the lead close home after she had headed him inside the final furlong. Before his trip to Chicago he had been successful in one of his four races as a five-year-old – the Pacemaker International Stakes for the second time. A confirmed front-runner and a horse of immense courage and determination, Teleprompter seemed well suited for the

Million, for he could produce early speed to hold his position on the tight bends, and his grit could be relied on to keep him going when attacked by his rivals.

With his regular jockey Tony Ives sporting the familiar colours of owner Lord Derby – black, white cap – he faced twelve opponents. There were two other British challengers: the filly Free Guest (whose trainer Luca Cumani had sent over Tolomeo to win in 1983), fresh from an easy victory in the Nassau Stakes at Goodwood, and Paul Mellon's King of Clubs, who had recently finished third in the Sussex Stakes at the same course. Seven of the ten American runners had earlier been based in Europe, including names familiar to English racegoers in Al Mamoon, Both Ends Burning, Drumalis and The Noble Player. Dahar, who had won the Prix Lupin at Longchamp in 1984 from the French stable of Maurice Zilber, was well fancied, as was Greinton, winner of six races as a two-year-old and three as a three-year-old when trained in France by François Boutin: now in the care of Charlie Whittingham in California, he had won the Hollywood Gold Cup and the California Stakes. Gate Dancer had won the Preakness in 1984 but had raced only once before on turf, and Tsunami Slew had taken the important Eddie Read Handicap at Del Mar. At the off Dahar and Greinton were both on 18–10, Gate Dancer on 43–10 and Free Guest on 54–10. Teleprompter started at a shade over 14–1.

A typical Chicago rainstorm the previous day had transformed the expected firm going to ground that was dead, and Teleprompter would not want it too soft. On the morning of the race the rain held off, but Teleprompter's draw raised another worry, for he was in the inside berth, and thus in danger of being shut off on the hectic run to the first bend, at the stands end of the home straight. But as soon as the gates flew open Bill Shoemaker and The Noble Player, drawn on Teleprompter's outside, pushed ahead without coming across to the rails, allowing Ives to boot the British-trained gelding into the lead and keep the vital rails berth. As Teleprompter's long, raking stride took the field round the clubhouse turn, Ives's first tactical point had been won, and in his wake Drumalis, Tsunami Slew and Free Guest led

## Budweiser Arlington Million

Arlington Park
1¼ miles
25 August 1985

| 1 | Teleprompter | T. Ives | 142–10 |
|---|---|---|---|
| 2 | Greinton | L. Pincay | 18–10 jt fav. |
| 3 | Flying Pidgeon | J. Santos | 301–10 |

*Also ran:* King Of Clubs (4th), The Noble Player, Al Mamoon, Tsunami Slew, Both Ends Burning, Dahar, Gate Dancer, Drumalis, Free Guest, Kings Island

13 ran

Winner owned by Lord Derby, trained by J. W. Watts

*Distances:* ¾ length, 3½ lengths

*... and his neck out. Greinton is second.*

the rest. After half a mile Ives, well aware that ten furlongs was on the long side for his mount, slowed the pace down a little, and the consequent bunching towards the rear of the field caused Greinton to be pulled sharply to the outside, twisting a hind shoe in the process. Coming to the far end of the back stretch and approaching the final bend Ives put his foot back on the gas and Teleprompter responded willingly with a surge off the bend and into the straight. Now, with less than two furlongs to go, he had put three lengths between himself and his rivals. Tsunami Slew and Free Guest could not cut back the deficit. The only possible danger was Greinton, and he was stuck behind a wall of horses, so jockey Laffit Pincay pulled him to the outside and set off after Teleprompter. He managed to cut down the gap considerably but Teleprompter would not be denied, and kept going resolutely to with-

stand Greinton's challenge by three-quarters of a length. Flying Pidgeon, one of the rank outsiders, was third, and King Of Clubs fourth.

In slightly over two minutes and three seconds Teleprompter netted five times what he had already won in Europe over four seasons. He thus became England's leading money-winner, but this record lasted only until Pebbles took the Breeders' Cup Turf – with Teleprompter about six lengths back in sixth place – two months later (see pages 79–81). He also became the first English-trained gelding to win a Group One or Grade One race anywhere in the world, providing British racing with one of its all-time high points on foreign soil. When he returned in triumph from Chicago to Richmond he posed for photographers beneath a huge banner: 'Welcome Home Teleprompter – One in a Million.'

# NIJINSKY

*King George VI and Queen Elizabeth Stakes*
*Ascot, 25 July 1970*

Nijinsky had the lot. Bred in Canada by E. P. Taylor, he boasted a superb pedigree, being a son of Northern Dancer out of the high-class racemare Flaming Page. He was sold for $84,000 (then a record for a Canadian-bred yearling), and his owner Charles Engelhard sent him to Ireland to be trained by Vincent O'Brien, under whose care he was unbeaten as a two-year-old, winning five races including the Dewhurst Stakes. (That his excellence did not exactly come as a surprise is indicated by his starting prices in these five races: 11–4 on, 9–4 on, 9–4 on, 7–2 on and 3–1

on.) He matured into a magnificent-looking three-year-old, tall, athletic and blessed with that *hauteur* which marked him out on looks as on breeding an aristocrat among horses.

And he turned in performances to match. He won the Gladness Stakes at The Curragh, beating a four-year-old named Deep Run, later to become a prolific sire of National Hunt winners. Next stop was Newmarket, where he took the Two Thousand Guineas with ease. In the Derby at Epsom (the only occasion he started at odds against) he beat the high-class French colt Gyr by two and a

*Nijinsky saunters in from Blakeney.*

Ascot
1½ miles
25 July 1970

| | | |
|---|---|---|
| 1 Nijinsky | L. Piggott | 40–85 fav. |
| 2 Blakeney | G. Lewis | 100–7 |
| 3 Crepellana | J. Deforge | 20–1 |

*Also ran:* Karabas (4th), Hogarth, Caliban

6 ran

Winner owned by C. W. Engelhard, trained by M. V. O'Brien

*Distances:* 2 lengths, 4 lengths

❛ *He was up against good older horses, and he still won in a canter* ❜

OPPOSITE *Trainer Vincent O'Brien leads in Nijinsky and Lester Piggott.*

half lengths, and then won the Irish Derby without fuss.

Lester Piggott had ridden the colt to his two English Classic wins, though stable jockey Liam Ward had taken over in the Irish Derby. Piggott was back in the saddle for Nijinsky's next race, the King George VI and Queen Elizabeth Stakes, which would be the first real opportunity to measure his worth against the best horses of the older generation. (Older horses had opposed him in the Gladness Stakes, but that was before his Classic victories.) The King George field – in which, unusually, Nijinsky was the only three-year-old – was small but select. Blakeney had won the Derby the previous year, and Hogarth the Italian Derby in 1968. Karabas had been ridden by Piggott to victory in the Washington International in 1969, Crepellana had won the Prix de Diane that year, and Caliban had taken the Coronation Cup the month before the King George. It was the strongest opposition Nijinsky had yet faced, but if he had any claims to be horse of the century, as some were already billing him, he had to win with ease. He started at 85–40 on to do so, with Caliban at 5–1, Karabas at 13–2, and Blakeney at 100–7: that any Derby winner should start at such a long price indicated the generally held view that the 1970 Derby victor was simply in a a different class from his immediate predecessor.

The Italian challenger Hogarth led for the first furlong before giving way to Caliban, who went on from Hogarth, Karabas, Blakeney and Nijinsky, with Crepellana bringing up the rear. The order remained much the same as they ran down into Swinley Bottom and made the long right-hand turn before beginning the climb towards the straight. At the turn for home Bill Williamson on Karabas came up to challenge Sandy Barclay on Caliban, with Hogarth trying to hold his place, Geoff Lewis keeping Blakeney to the inside and Piggott still motionless on Nijinsky. Two furlongs out Caliban started to weaken and Karabas took a slight lead from Hogarth, with Blakeney making his move up the rail, but with a furlong and a half to go Piggott decided that it was about time to make his move. He switched Nijinksy to the middle of the course and shook him up briefly. The response was electric, as Nijin-sky brought into play his supreme quality of instant acceleration and sprinted away from the others. This surge took him far enough clear for Piggott to allow himself a languid look round at his toiling rivals, and his mount was so superior that he eased up: this brought Blakeney slightly too close for comfort, and Piggott had to push Nijinsky out for a couple of strides before the line. He won, without being extended, by two lengths, with Crepellana running on to take third place a further four lengths away.

Although Nijinsky had done no more than had been widely expected of him, it was none the less a dazzling performance, and it confirmed his marked superiority not only over his own age-group but over the best that the older generations could throw at him. In his next race he became the first horse since Bahram in 1935 to take the Triple Crown when cantering to success in the St Leger at Doncaster, but he had suffered a fierce attack of ringworm during his preparation for that race and lost an abnormal amount of weight through his exertions. Although it was not fully appreciated at the time, he had not made a complete recovery before the Prix de l'Arc de Triomphe at Longchamp in early October, which probably explains his head defeat by Sassafras as much as the immediate reaction that Piggott had ridden an ill-judged race in expecting the horse to make up too much ground in the short Longchamp straight. The bid to end Nijinsky's racing career on a winning note by taking in the Champion Stakes at Newmarket ended in deep disappointment as he failed to get to Lorenzaccio – a horse not in Nijinsky's league on his best form – and was beaten one and a half lengths. He was then retired to stud, where his offspring have included the Derby winners Golden Fleece and Shahrastani.

If Nijinsky's last two appearances were an anti-climax, they do not dilute the heady memory of this wonderful horse at his peak, and the zenith of his racecourse career was surely at Ascot. 'The King George VI Stakes was probably Nijinsky's best race ever,' said Lester Piggott, 'because he was up against good older horses and he still won in a canter. The race was really a formality. I have never been more impressed with a horse.'

*Mill Reef goes clear of Pistol Packer.*

❡ *Comme Sea Bird II –*
*mais plus vite* ❡

By the time Mill Reef was flown to Paris for the Prix de l'Arc de Triomphe, Paul Mellon's three-year-old colt had already shown himself to be the best middle-distance horse in Europe. After a three-length defeat by Brigadier Gerard in the Two Thousand Guineas (see pages 20–3) he had won the Derby, the Eclipse Stakes and the King George VI and Queen Elizabeth Stakes, and he was a hot favourite to become the first English-trained horse to win the Arc since Migoli's victory in 1948. Ridden by Geoff Lewis, who had taken the Prix de l'Abbaye on Sweet Revenge earlier in the afternoon, he faced seventeen opponents. Of the French home team, the three-

year-old filly Pistol Packer had won the Prix de Diane by a short head from Cambrizzia (also running in the Arc); she had beaten Cambrizzia again in the Prix de la Nonette and in the Prix Vermeille at Longchamp. The field also included the French-based Caro, a soundly beaten second to Mill Reef in the Eclipse, Miss Dan, two lengths behind Nijinsky when third in the Arc in 1970, Bourbon, who had won the Prix Royal-Oak (the French St Leger) and Irish Ball, who, though third to Mill Reef in the Derby and unplaced in the King George, had between those two races won the Irish Derby at The Curragh. Also representing France were Ramsin, who had won the Prix du Cadran and the Grand

*Mill Reef at the National Stud in Newmarket.*

Prix de Saint-Cloud, and his stable-companion Arlequino, winner of the Prix de Chantilly. From the USA came One For All, who had won over $300,000 but was a distinct outsider in Europe's top race. The only English-trained horses pitched in against Mill Reef were Ortis, second in the King George after winning the Hardwicke Stakes at Royal Ascot, and the three-year-old Royalty, unbeaten but untried in high-class company.

A hefty contingent of English spectators had made the trip to Paris to support Mill Reef, and at the off his price on the Pari-Mutuel was 10–7 on. Pistol Packer and Bourbon were coupled on 17–4, with Arlequino, Ramsin and his pacemaker Ossian on 7–1. No other horse started at less than 20–1.

First out of the stalls was the American challenger One For All, but then Ossian took up his pacemaking role and led along the far side from Ramsin and the Aga Khan's Sharapour. Mill Reef was about sixth, with Pistol Packer towards the rear. At the top of the hill

Ossian still had the lead, and he kept in front as the runners made down to the final bend, though Pistol Packer and Caro were improving their positions. Once in the straight Ossian surrendered to Sharapour and Ortis, then Lester Piggott on Hallez came to the front. As Sharapour fell back it seemed for a moment as if he would get in the way of Mill Reef on the rails, but Lewis was alert to the perils of getting boxed in up the short Longchamp straight and pulled Mill Reef out to begin his challenge. One smack with the whip – the first time that Mill Reef had received such encouragement since the Guineas – and he was through a gap between Hallez and Ortis with less than two furlongs to race. Meanwhile Pistol Packer was getting into top gear on the stands side, and Caro and Arlequino were not done with. But a furlong out Mill Reef had sprinted clear, and only Pistol Packer could deny him the greatest moment of an outstanding racing career. She got to his tail, but then in the final hundred yards Mill Reef produced a fresh surge of power and trebled his advantage. At the post he was three lengths to the good, with Cambrizzia running on to be third. Caro was a neck further back in fourth.

Mill Reef's victory had proved him one of the greatest European racehorses of the age. He received a tumultuous welcome on returning to unsaddle, and when the dust settled the plaudits rained down. Freddie Head, rider of Pistol Packer, opined that 'Mill Reef was the best horse I've ever seen', and the French press compared him with the horse whose stunning victory in the Arc six years earlier had marked him out as the very best horse of the era: *'Comme Sea Bird II - mais plus vite'*, raved *Paris-Turf*. He was indeed *plus vite*, for his Arc time of 2 minutes 28.3 seconds set a new course record.

Mill Reef returned to Longchamp the following spring to notch up a ten-length victory in the Prix Ganay, but after a lacklustre display when beating Homeric a neck in the Coronation Cup at Epsom he did not race again: he was being prepared for a second Arc when on 30 August 1972 he fractured a foreleg on the gallops, and was retired to stud. He was put down early in 1986 at the age of eighteen when an incurable heart condition was diagnosed.

# DANCING BRAVE

*Prix de l'Arc de Triomphe*
*Longchamp, 5 October 1986*

*Dancing Brave surges past Bering (black sleeves), Triptych (no. 9) and Shardari (brown cap)...*

The tidal wave of Dancing Brave's progress up the Longchamp straight to win the 1986 Prix de l'Arc de Triomphe provided the greatest moment of European Flat racing in the 1980s. And though the winner was US-bred, owned by a Saudi Arabian prince and ridden by an Irish-born jockey, this was a moment of the utmost sweetness for British racing, for Dancing Brave, here proving himself the horse of the decade by treating with contempt an international field of the highest quality, was trained in Sussex by Guy Harwood.

Such was the speed that Dancing Brave showed when winning the General Accident Two Thousand Guineas at Newmarket that some felt that the Derby – half a mile longer than the Guineas – might not be his race, but he took his chance at Epsom and started 2–1

favourite. He was beaten half a length in probably the most controversial big Flat race run in England in the 1980s. Greville Starkey's riding of the horse came in for fierce criticism, but he made no mistake in Dancing Brave's next race, drawing right away from Triptych to win the Coral-Eclipse Stakes at Sandown Park. However, Pat Eddery replaced the injured Starkey for the King George VI and Queen Elizabeth Diamond Stakes, where revenge was taken on Shahrastani, beaten into fourth as Dancing Brave disposed of Shardari and Triptych. One warm-up race at Goodwood (for which Dancing Brave was such a certainty that the bookmakers returned no starting price), and it was off to his appointment with greatness in the Arc.

The field for the 1986 Prix de l'Arc de Triomphe was the strongest the race had

**Trusthouse Forte Prix de l'Arc de Triomphe**

Longchamp
2400 metres
5 October 1986

| 1 | Dancing Brave | P. Eddery | 11–10 fav. |
| 2 | Bering | G. Moore | 11–4 |
| 3 | Triptych | A. Cordero | 64–1 |

*Also ran:* Shahrastani (4th), Shardari, Darara, Acatenango, Mersey, Saint Estephe, Dihistan, Iades, Baby Turk, Nemain, Sirius Symboli, Maria Fumata

15 ran

Winner owned by K. Abdullah, trained by G. Harwood

*Distances:* 1½ lengths, ½ length

offered for years, adding up to the most valuable collection of bloodstock ever assembled for a single race in Europe. Apart from Dancing Brave, the three-year-old generation was represented by the Derby winner Shahrastani, by the filly Darara, who had recently won the Trusthouse Forte Prix Vermeille, one of France's top races for three-year-old fillies, and by Bering, unbeaten in four races that season including the Prix du Jockey-Club Lancia (the French equivalent of the Derby). There was the ubiquitous Triptych, now a four-year-old: she had won only one race in the 1986 season but had been placed in the Coronation Cup (beaten a short head by Saint Estephe), the Coral-Eclipse Stakes, the King George, the Matchmaker International at York (beaten threequarters of a length by Shardari) and the Phoenix Champion Stakes (third to

Park Express). In the Arc she was reopposed by Shardari and by Saint Estephe, who had himself been beaten in the Grand Prix de Saint-Cloud by the German-trained Acatenango, also in the Longchamp field and unbeaten in his last twelve races, including the German Derby. Mersey had won the Prix Royal-Oak (the French St Leger) in 1985; Iades had won the Prix Dollar at Chantilly; Baby Turk had won the Grand Prix de Deauville. That Dihistan, who had won the Hardwicke Stakes at Royal Ascot, was in the race as pacemaker for Shahrastani and Shardari, bears witness to the class of the race.

Well backed by the huge number of British racegoers who had flocked to the Arc on the first Sunday in October, Dancing Brave started at odds of 11–10 on the Pari-Mutuel to beat his fourteen opponents, with Bering second favourite at 11–4. The going was

*. and goes clear.*

*Dancing Brave (Pat Eddery) in the parade.*

firm. In the early stages both Pat Eddery on Dancing Brave and Gary Moore on Bering held up their mounts towards the rear, but had improved to the middle of the pack as the field made the downhill run towards the straight. At the turn for home Baby Turk led from Nemain and Acatenango, but behind them the four runners owned by the Aga Khan – Shardari, Dihistan, Darara and Shahrastani – were making their efforts, and over a quarter of a mile out Shardari hit the front, closely pursued by Shahrastani and Darara. Then Bering got into top gear and swept past the Aga Khan's runners, taking it up from Shahrastani inside the final furlong. It was a surge of acceleration which in any normal race would have ensured victory, but this was no normal race: suddenly Dancing Brave was there, charging up the middle of the track with a relentless power. One moment halfway up the straight it looked as if Eddery might have cut it too fine; the next

it was a question of how far he would win by, for this burst of speed was so decisive that it made the top horses in Europe look one-paced. It proclaimed Dancing Brave one of the great horses of the century.

The official winning margin over Bering was one and a half lengths. Triptych ran a marvellous race, making up a vast amount of ground in the straight to finish third. The time for the race was a course record.

The following day it was revealed that Bering had chipped a bone in a knee during the race, but such was the power of his acceleration as he took up the running that he could hardly have been affected until the very final stages.

Sadly Dancing Brave's career ended in anti-climax. Sent to Santa Anita in California for the Breeders' Cup Turf a month later, he could only manage fourth behind Manila, Theatrical and Estrapade. He was then retired to stud.

# CRISP AND RED RUM

*Grand National*
*Liverpool, 31 March 1973*

❝ *I'm afraid, Sir Chester, we are going to be beaten* ❞

The 1973 Grand National was won by Red Rum, ridden by Brian Fletcher, by three quarters of a length from Crisp, with L'Escargot twenty-five lengths away in third and Spanish Steps a further twelve lengths back in fourth. Those are the facts. But somehow they are wrong, for at every stage of this incredible race – at every stage, that is, bar the one that matters, at the winning post – the only rightful winner had to be Crisp, whose astonishing display of galloping and jumping in the toughest race in the calendar must, were there any justice in the world, have been blessed with success.

Thirty-eight runners went to post, with Red Rum and Crisp joint favourites at 9–1. Red Rum was an eight-year-old, and had had to work hard for his corn, being trained in several yards and shrugging off the effects of damaging foot disease, before finding his true vocation in the care of trainer Ginger McCain, who bought Red Rum for 6000 guineas on behalf of owner Noel Le Mare, and gradually made the horse into one of the best chasers in the north; he owed his position in the Grand National betting to highly encouraging runs in three handicaps early in 1973 following five successive victories the previous autumn.

Among his main rivals were L'Escargot, who had won the Cheltenham Gold Cup in 1970 and 1971, the 1972 Whitbread Gold Cup winner Grey Sombrero, the high-class chaser Spanish Steps – and Crisp, who in the National carried joint top weight of twelve stone with L'Escargot. Spanish Steps carried one pound less. Red Rum was saddled with a mere ten stone five pounds. Bred in Australia by his owner Sir Chester Manifold, Crisp had come to Britain in 1970 to be trained by Fred Winter. He won his first race at Wincanton in brilliant style and then took the top two-mile chase of the season – the Champion Chase at the Cheltenham National Hunt Festival in 1971 – by twenty-five lengths. The following season he was back at the Festival as favourite for the Gold Cup, but soft going and the distance of three and a quarter miles proved his undoing, and he finished fifth. In 1973 he again tried his hand at Cheltenham and ran third in the Champion Chase before being directed to Liverpool for the Grand National. This seemed a race well

beyond his stamina range, for the Grand National is over nearly four and a half miles and Crisp's ideal distance was apparently no further than two and a half miles. On the other hand, his jumping was superb, and the thirty formidable fences of the National course would hold no terrors for him. He was a chaser of the highest class, and had not other horses of unproven stamina excelled themselves in the National?

From the moment the tapes rose Crisp was in the front rank, and by the time the field swept over Becher's Brook – the sixth fence – he was sharing the lead with Grey Sombrero. Two fences later, as the runners swerved left over the Canal Turn, he had sped to the front and was inexorably increasing his advantage and turning the Grand National into a glorious exhibition round. He gambolled over the four fences on the run towards the turn for home on the first circuit, and made towards the stands with a commanding lead. He bounded over the thirteenth and fourteenth and set off for the Chair, that huge open ditch which forms the biggest obstacle on the course. By now he was some twenty lengths in front of his pursuers, and it was becoming a matter of how long this horse of doubtful stamina could keep going. At the Chair he pricked his ears and sailed over the gaping ditch with such abandon that he pecked slightly on the landing side. But he recovered his balance in a stride and made off for the water jump. Behind him Grey Sombrero took a crashing fall at the Chair and broke his shoulder, but all eyes were on Crisp as he skipped over the water in front of the exhilarated spectators in the stands and swung out towards the second circuit.

His lead now was enormous. The pursuers were keeping up as best they could but held little hope of catching him, though at the first fence on the second circuit – the seventeenth in the race – Red Rum could be seen to be keeping on gamely. But Crisp was still way ahead, disdaining his top weight and jumping with a breathtaking fluency. At the nineteenth, a big open ditch, he stood back and put in an extravagant leap: he still had plenty of gas in the tank. Way behind him Red Rum had moved into second. Crisp was putting in an astounding performance. 'I

LEFT *Crisp and Richard Pitman at the Grand National start on the morning of the race.*

*Crisp soars over Becher's Brook on the second circuit.*

can't remember a horse so far ahead in the Grand National at this stage!' enthused commentator Julian Wilson on BBC television as Crisp came to Becher's Brook for the second time, still looking uncatchable: galloping relentlessly and jumping brilliantly, he was thirty lengths clear and showed no signs of flagging. This would be the most spectacular victory in the history of the great race. He took the Canal Turn as fluently as he had on the first circuit, then swept towards Valentine's Brook. Now there was only one possible danger – Red Rum, a long way in arrears but slowly, very slowly, getting closer. Six fences from home, and the winner could still only be Crisp. Five from home, four and

three – the nearer the finish came, the more certain his victory seemed to be. Richard Pitman stole a quick look round to assess the closeness of his nearest pursuer – at least twenty lengths – and shortened the reins to keep Crisp together for the final draining half mile. He was still going well enough, but then, as he turned towards the stands for the last time, a doubt began to nibble, and then to gnaw. Was he losing his momentum? Brian Fletcher on Red Rum thought he was, and urged his mount to keep up the pursuit. The gap was surely closing, and Crisp was not home yet. At the second last fence Crisp was still ten lengths to the good but he was clearly coming to the end of his tether. After

## Grand National

Liverpool
4 miles 865 yards
31 March 1973

| | | |
|---|---|---|
| 1 Red Rum | B. Fletcher | 9–1 jt fav. |
| 2 Crisp | R. Pitman | 9–1 jt fav. |
| 3 L'Escargot | T. Carberry | 11–1 |

*Also ran:* Spanish Steps (4th), Rouge
Autumn, Hurricane Rock, Proud Tarquin,
Prophecy, Endless Folly, Black Secret,
Petruchio's Son, The Pooka, Great Noise,
Green Plover, Sunny Lad, Go-Pontinental,
Mill Door, Grey Sombrero, Glenkiln,
Beggar's Way, Ashville, Tarquin Bid,
Richeleau, Charley Winking, Proud Percy,
Culla Hill, Canharis, Fortune Bay, Swan-Shot,
General Symons, Highland Seal, Mr Vimy,
Astbury, Beau Parc, Rough Silk, Princess
Camilla, Rampsman, Nereo

38 ran

Winner owned by N. H. Le Mare, trained by
D. McCain

*Distances:* ¾ length, 25 lengths

OPPOSITE *Norton's Coin is led
from the unsaddling enclosure
after the Tote Cheltenham Gold
Cup, March 1990.*

BELOW *Red Rum (left) catches
Crisp just before the winning
post.*

the second last Pitman sneaked another look behind him, and this telegraphed to Brian Fletcher that all was not lost. As Crisp, tiring with every stride, made for the thirtieth and final fence the awful prospect of defeat loomed large. He was losing his action, and beginning to roll around with fatigue. Could he last home? Trainer Fred Winter had watched the race with Crisp's owner Sir Chester Manifold without uttering a word, but now, as their horse plugged gallantly on, he announced, 'I'm afraid, Sir Chester, we are going to be beaten.'

At the last fence Crisp, though he walloped the gorse into the air, still held a substantial lead, but Red Rum – with twenty-three pounds less on his back – was charging along now, and it was simply a matter of whether Crisp could survive the desperately long run to the winning post. Coming to the Elbow, where the runners veer right-handed off the main course towards the line with little more than a furlong to go, Pitman gave his mount a smack down the right-hand side. Crisp, out on his feet staggered away to the left. Pitman yanked him back on to a true line and managed to steer him clear of the rails, but the two hundred yards he had left to run seemed like two hundred miles, and Red Rum was now only five lengths back. Crisp had slowed almost to a trot, but still it seemed that he might hold on. Richard Pitman describes

those gut-wrenching moments:

*No longer was Crisp's action light and
forward, it was now laboured and
sideways as if he was drunk. The tell-
tale noises were close, but so was the
winning post – or was it? It almost
seemed as if it was moving further away
with each stride.*

*With only fifteen yards to go Crisp
tightened as he felt Red Rum's presence
but it was his dying effort and only
lasted for a second. Two strides away
from the post Red Rum's head forged
past my gallant partner to snatch
victory from our grasp.*

Red Rum had won. Crisp had lost. L'Escargot was third, Spanish Steps fourth. The time for the race – 9 minutes 1.9 seconds – beat the previous record (Golden Miller in 1934) by nearly twenty seconds and was to stand until 1990. Beneath those facts lie the high emotion, the drama, the fever-pitch excitement, the *wrong* of this extraordinary race. For although Red Rum went on to win two more Grand Nationals in 1974 and 1977 (and to finish second in the intervening years of 1975 and 1976), and although Crisp beat Red Rum easily the next time they met, there has never been a big race which a beaten horse so deserved to win. Red Rum may have won the race, but never mind the facts. This will always be Crisp's Grand National.

# A SENSE OF OCCASION

# DEVON LOCH

*Grand National*
*Liverpool, 24 March 1956*

TOP *Devon Loch (black cap) swings over second Becher's just behind E.S.B. and the falling Sundew.*

ABOVE *The Royal Party at the instant of Devon Loch's leaping into the air. Some catch on more quickly than others, and some aren't watching the race at all.*

Poor Devon Loch. The fate that befell him in the 1956 Grand National booked him a permanent place not only in the reminiscences of racing folk but in the British national memory. For he was the Queen Mother's steeplechaser who belly-flopped yards from the Grand National winning post, the horse who grabbed defeat from the very jaws of victory in such a way that even those with no interest whatsoever in the sport of racing still recall the sight of 'that horse who jumped the fence that wasn't there'.

Since the late 1940s the Queen Mother had been the darling of National Hunt rac-ing: it was largely her enthusiasm for the sport that raised its status from that of a poor relation to the Flat to, by the mid-1950s, a position of near equality – in popularity if not in the prize money available. She had owned good horses such as Manicou (who had won the King George VI Chase in 1950) and Monaveen (who had finished fifth to Freebooter in that year's Grand National as his royal owner's first runner in the race), but in Devon Loch she had a chaser who ap-parently had all the attributes to win her the greatest steeplechase in the calendar: he was a big horse, strongly built and bold yet intel-ligent enough to look after himself in the hurly-burly of four and half miles and thirty fences. In December 1954 he was ridden for the first time by the reigning champion jockey Dick Francis: after the race Francis told Cazalet that he would like to ride Devon Loch one day in the Grand National ...

The New Century Chase at Hurst Park in February 1955 marked Devon Loch's first victory in the colours of his royal owner – blue, buff stripes, blue sleeves, black cap, gold tassel – and he won once more that sea-son, beating a future Cheltenham Gold Cup winner in Linwell. By the spring of 1956 Devon Loch, now a ten-year-old but lightly raced, was clearly a serious candidate for the Grand National: he had won two good chases the previous autumn and finished fifth in the King George VI Chase to Limber Hill. He then ran a gallant race when third to Linwell in the Mildmay Memorial Chase over three miles five furlongs at Sandown Park, conceding twenty-three pounds to the winner and finishing only one and a half lengths behind him. Dick Francis was side-lined through injury, and Bryan Marshall, who rode the horse in the King George and the Mildmay, informed Cazalet that on both occasions his mount had seemed to falter halfway through the race, before finding his second wind and running on again. This quirk was to come under scrutiny in the Liverpool post-mortems a few months later.

In his pre-National race Devon Loch gave a stone to another future Gold Cup winner, Kerstin, when running third to her in the National Hunt Chase at Cheltenham, after which Dick Francis reported to the Queen Mother that 'Devon Loch was staying on

*As the newsreel saw it: Devon Loch collapses, then struggles to his feet as E.S.B. comes past.*

❝ *The calamity which overtook us was sudden, terrible, and completely without warning* ❞

related in his autobiography *The Sport of Queens*: 'I have never ridden another horse like him. He cleared the formidable Aintree fences as easily as if they had been hurdles. He put himself right before every one of them, and he was so intelligent at the job that all I had to do was to ride him quietly and let him jump without fussing him.' (It is worth remembering that in those days the Grand National fences did not incorporate a sloping apron of gorse on the take-off side to help the horses jump accurately: the take-off side was sheer, and consequently more difficult to gauge correctly.) The longer the race went on, the better Devon Loch jumped, and as he soared over Becher's Brook on the second circuit no runner was going better: the Queen Mother's dream of winning the Grand National was about to come true. By the Canal Turn he was second, and he kept up his gallop as the field came back towards the stands, taking up the running with three fences to go. His only serious challenger was E.S.B., but Devon Loch was a length to the good at the last fence and started to pull away up the run-in, over a quarter of a mile long. E.S.B. was dead tired and Dave Dick had accepted that he would not win, for Devon Loch was scooting along, increasing his lead and certain to land a famous and hugely popular victory. The crowd was wild with excitement. Hats were in the air. Here was the most loved owner in British racing, the most adored individual in British society, about to win the country's greatest steeplechase – a fitting reward for all that she had put into the sport. Devon Loch had a hundred yards to go, ninety, eighty, seventy, sixty. Twelve strides and he would be home – eleven, ten …

The next heart-stopping moment can only be properly described in the jockey's own words:

*In one stride he was bounding smoothly along, a poem of controlled motion; in the next, his hind legs stiffened and refused to function. He fell flat on his belly, his limbs splayed out sideways and backwards in unnatural angles, and when he stood up he could hardly move … the rhythm was shattered, the dream was over, and the race was lost.*

really well, and I feel we have a great chance at Aintree.' On National day the bookmakers assessed his chance at 100–7, with Must the favourite and Sundew (who was to win the race the following year) second favourite. Also in the field of twenty-nine were previous winners Early Mist (1953) and Royal Tan, who at the age of twelve started at 28–1 to repeat his 1954 victory. Bracketed with Devon Loch at 100–7 was E.S.B., trained by Fred Rimell and ridden by Dave Dick, and the Queen Mother ran a second string in M'as-tu-vu, ridden by Arthur Freeman.

The bulk of the race does not need much describing. Suffice it to say that Devon Loch gave Dick Francis a dream ride, as the jockey

*A bewildered Dick Francis walks back to the weighing room as Devon Loch is led away.*

## Grand National

Liverpool
4 miles 856 yards
24 March 1956

| 1 E.S.B. | D. V. Dick | 100–7 |
| 2 Gentle Moya | G. Milburn | 22–1 |
| 3 Royal Tan | T. Taaffe | 28–1 |

*Also ran:* Eagle Lodge (4th), Key Royal, Martinique, Carey's Cottage, Clearing, Wild Wisdom, Early Mist, Mariner's Log, Devon Loch, Sundew, High Guard, Much Obliged, Dunboy, Armorial III, Merry Windsor, Must, M'as-tu-vu, Reverend Prince, Witty, Domata, Polonius, Athenian, No Response, Ontray, Border Luck, Pippykin

29 ran

Winner owned by Mrs L. Carver, trained by T. F. Rimell

*Distances:* 10 lengths, 10 lengths

To the massed spectators in the stands, flung in an instant from joyous acclaim of a Royal winner to horrified, dumbfounded silence, Devon Loch had seemed to leap at an imaginary obstacle before slithering to the ground and skidding along to a halt, the momentum throwing Francis up on to the horse's neck. As Devon Loch struggled up there was still time for him to get going again and hold off E.S.B., but his hind legs seemed not to function and he could not move on. E.S.B. went by him to register a ten-length victory from Gentle Moya, with Royal Tan another ten lengths away third, but all eyes — stunned, disbelieving eyes — were on the stricken Devon Loch as Dick Francis slid off his back. Peter Cazalet's travelling head lad rushed on to the course to lead the horse away as a bemused jockey was taken back to the weighing room. The Queen Mother and Cazalet went over to see Devon Loch and he appeared to be sound: inspection by a vet immediately after the calamity revealed nothing amiss with him.

The most sensational collapse in the history of British racing has never been conclusively explained, though many theories were advanced. Devon Loch had appeared to take off right by the water jump, which the runners on the second circuit of the Grand National by-pass as they approach the winning post: had he caught that fence out of the corner of his eye and tried to jump it? Close examination of the film shows that he took off well before it; he was not under pressure and had no apparent reason to panic. Some thought he had suffered a momentary heart problem, but he was not running like a tired horse and afterwards was completely sound. Perhaps he had hit a patch of false going which caused him to lose his action, or had a fleeting muscular spasm which lost him the use of his hind legs — something like Bryan Marshall had reported after a couple of his races earlier in the season.

Probably the clue to the most plausible explanation — and the one put forward by the man most likely to know, his jockey Dick Francis — lies in the fact that just before he slid to the ground Devon Loch pricked his ears, in the way that a horse might do just before jumping a fence — or on suddenly hearing an unfamiliar noise. Certainly what Devon Loch heard at that moment was not a noise which he had heard before, and it was some noise — a raucous surge of patriotic fervour as the Royal horse galloped to certain victory in front of his owner the Queen Mother and her daughters Queen Elizabeth II and Princess Margaret, a rapturous climax befitting what was about to be one of the greatest moments of racing history. Francis wrote that 'the cheering was incredible':

*I have never heard in my life such a noise. It rolled and lapped around us, buffeting and glorious, the enthusiastic expression of love for the Royal family and delight in seeing the Royal horse win.*

The Grand National course narrows approaching the winning post and bends round to the left immediately after, and with crowds manically screaming at him in the stands and on both rails and directly in front of him it would hardly be surprising if Devon Loch had suddenly been startled by the deafening noise. Perhaps he stopped simply because he was scared.

The Queen Mother took the reverse stoically, writing to Cazalet a few days after the Grand National: 'We will not be done in by this, and will just keep on trying.' The only creature who could explain what had happened was Devon Loch, and he was not in a position to give interviews. To this day Devon Loch's collapse remains one of the Turf's greatest unsolved mysteries.

# EMILY DAVISON, ANMER AND ABOYEUR

*Derby Stakes*
*Epsom, 4 June 1913*

*◀ The abominable behaviour of a brutal, lunatic woman ▶*

On rising ground at the western end of the churchyard of St Mary's at Morpeth in Northumberland stands, sheltered by cedar trees, a funerary monument. This is the last resting place of the local Davison family, and under the name Emily Wilding Davison, born 11 October 1872, died 8 June 1913, is inscribed the phrase 'Deeds, not words'. Whether she intended it or not, Emily's deed during the 1913 Derby at Epsom afforded her the status of martyr, and her grave was to become a shrine.

Events in the race itself summon up less pious images, for this running of the world's greatest Classic saw a brawling match up the straight and a sensational disqualification which to many smelled of more than one personal vendetta. And for plenty of people, now as then, Emily Davison was not a martyr but an obsessive fanatic whose activities brought no credit to her cause and whose action on Derby Day 1913 was that of a hooligan, not a heroine. No one emerged from the day with much distinction.

Emily Davison was among the most militant members of the Women's Social and Political Union – the suffragettes. Soon after joining the WSPU in 1906 she had embarked on a campaign of disruptive action which by the time she went to Epsom for the Derby had brought her numerous prison sentences for offences such as obstruction, throwing bricks, setting fire to pillar-boxes and smashing windows in the House of Commons. (She had attacked a man in Aberdeen in the mistaken notion that he was Lloyd George: in fact he was a Baptist minister.) At the end of May 1913 Emily Davison was at home in Longhorsley, near Morpeth, recovering from her latest spell in prison, when she received by telegram the instructions that took her to Tattenham Corner as the Derby field approached.

It is not known who sent the instructions, nor exactly what they were. What is certain is that on the bright and sunny morning of 4 June 1913 the forty-year-old Emily Davison called at the offices of the WSPU in London and asked for two of the union's white, green and purple flags. One she carried tightly rolled up in her hand; the other she pinned inside her coat. She then went to Victoria

Station and bought a return ticket to Epsom, where she took up a position in the pressing crowd on the inside rails at Tattenham Corner, a few yards before the runners reach the straight.

Fifteen horses were competing that year for a first prize in the Derby of £6450. The hot favourite at 6–4 was Craganour. He had apparently been a most unlucky loser of the Two Thousand Guineas at Newmarket, when the judge Charles Robinson had called Louvois the winner despite the conviction of most people present that Craganour, finishing on the other side of the course from his rival, had held on. Bill Saxby, who had ridden Craganour in the Guineas, lost the ride to Danny Maher for the colt's winning run in the Newmarket Stakes, and in the Derby rode Louvois, joint third favourite with the French challenger Nimbus. But Maher could not ride Craganour in the Derby as he had been claimed for Lord Rosebery's Prue, and the favourite was partnered by the American jockey Johnny Reiff. Second favourite Shogun at 6–1 was the only horse apart from Craganour to start at less than 10–1; King George V's horse Anmer, ridden by Herbert Jones, was 50–1. Among four horses on 100–1 was Aboyeur, the mount of Edwin Piper and a forlorn hope in the world's greatest Classic: he had won once from three runs as a two-year-old and been unplaced at Kempton Park on his only previous outing at three. To all appearances Aboyeur was a no-hoper and Craganour a certainty.

But Aboyeur's blinkered head showed in front soon after the start as he took the field along from Craganour and Aldegond, with Shogun, Nimbus and Louvois all handy. With a mile to run the King's colt Anmer was struggling to stay with the pace and started to drop back, and as the runners came down the hill Aboyeur was three lengths to the good, with Craganour, Day Comet, Shogun and Louvois best of the rest. At the rear Agadir and Anmer headed the stragglers but were both lost causes.

In position at Tattenham Corner, Emily Davison waited until the leading batch of horses had thundered past, then quickly squeezed through the crowd and under the rails on to the course. She managed to avoid

*Anmer, Herbert Jones and Emily
Davison crash to the ground.*

Agadir but then Anmer was upon her. She
held out her arms and tried desperately to
grab at Jones's reins, but three quarters of a
ton of racehorse hit her head-on at nearly
forty miles an hour and the three went down
in a heap. The playwright St John Ervine was
standing nearby and described what he saw
to the *Daily Mail*:

> *Miss Davison, who was standing close
> to the rails a few yards from me,
> suddenly ducked under the railings as
> the horses came up. The King's horse,
> Anmer, came up and Miss Davison went
> towards it. She put up her hand, but
> whether it was to catch hold of the reins
> or to protect herself, I do not know. It
> was over in a few seconds. The horse
> knocked the woman over with very
> great force, and then stumbled and fell,
> pitching the jockey violently onto the
> ground. Both he and Miss Davison were
> bleeding profusely.*

Another eyewitness, quoted in the *Daily
Sketch*, recounted:

> *Like a rabbit she ran across the course to
> intercept Anmer and as the horse was
> hugging the rails she stood up in front
> of him holding both her hands above
> her head, and then sprang at him. She
> caught the reins or bridle in her hands,
> and there hung suspended for a second
> as Anmer rushed on at a speed of over
> thirty miles an hour. Then the horse
> plunged as Jones shook the reins to get
> rid of the swaying woman, who still
> hung like a limpet, and Anmer rolled
> over towards the inside rails with Jones
> underneath. The woman was hurled
> clear and fell onto her side near the
> horse's flanks.*

It is important to take into consideration
more than one eye-witness report of these
few seconds (and the Gaumont newsreel
film) in an effort to decide what did happen;
but no account or film can tell us exactly

what Emily Davison's motive was. Eight
decades later the incident still causes dis-
cussion and disagreement, and opinions
vary about just what she intended to do. The
most likely explanation is that she intended
some disruption of the race and, having
ducked under the rails, found herself the
beneficiary of the sheer coincidence of the
King's horse – whose colours she would
have recognized – being isolated from the
other runners. It would seem that she intended to pull him down – in itself a tall
order – and so grabbed at the reins. But no
explanation of the most horrendous
moment in the history of the Derby can be
other than speculation.

As the crowds at Tattenham Corner
pushed under the rails to reach the stricken
pair the race itself was developing into a
barging match. Aboyeur was on the inside
with Craganour mounting an effective challenge on the stands side, and Nimbus, Great
Sport, Louvois, Shogun and Day Comet on
the heels of the leading pair. Shogun, having
come off best in a bout of shoving with Day
Comet, was making ground up the rails
when Reiff moved Craganour over to lean on
Aboyeur, causing the outsider to swerve to
the left and cut off Shogun's run on the
inside. Again Frank Wootton on Shogun
tried to get through, and again Aboyeur cut
him off. Now Craganour had gone half a
length up, but Aboyeur fought back as Piper
sought to straighten him by taking his whip
in his left hand and applying it liberally. But
this caused Aboyeur to veer away from the
rails and collide with Craganour, carrying
him out towards the centre of the course
and interfering with the finishing runs of
Nimbus – who had been far enough back at
Tattenham Corner for his jockey to have
seen the suffragette incident – and Great
Sport, both coming up the stands side. Reiff
retaliated by trying to push the favourite
back on to Aboyeur, and as the two went
past the post Craganour was a head up, with
Louvois just behind in third and Great Sport

Aboyeur (blinkers) fails by a head to push his way past Craganour (light cap).

fourth. There is good photographic evidence to suggest that Day Comet did in fact finish third, but the Epsom judge that day was the same Charles Robinson who had controversially denied Craganour the Two Thousand Guineas, and he placed Day Comet fifth.

Although there had clearly been a great deal of bumping and brawling, Aboyeur's jockey Edwin Piper declared on unsaddling that he had would not object. The 'All Right' signal was given from the weighing room and the red flag hoisted to confirm that the result stood. But a moment later, as Craganour was being led away, the 'All Right' decision was rescinded and the winner called back: the sensational news spread across the Downs that the Stewards themselves had objected to Craganour on the charge of jostling the second, Aboyeur. Initially few believed that the favourite would lose the race, for the scrimmaging had clearly been caused by both parties, and odds of 4–1 were laid against the outsider getting the race. But as time passed and the Stewards had still not delivered their decision it became obvious that the matter was not so clear-cut. Two of the Stewards, Lord Wolverton and Major Eustace Loder, interviewed the jockeys concerned in the finish; the third, Lord Rosebery, did not take part in the adjudication as he had a runner in the race. After a long period of deliberation, during which Craganour's owner Charles Bower Ismay was seen to become ever more pale, the official announcement was given: the race went to Aboyeur.

Was there a hidden agenda behind this decision? Eustace Loder, the prime mover of the Stewards' objection, was said to have a personal grudge against Craganour's owner Ismay, who in any case was far from universally popular: the son of the founder of the White Star Line, whose greatest ship the *Titanic* had gone down on its maiden voyage in 1912 with the loss of 1,517 lives, and himself a passenger on that fateful voyage, his survival did not endear

him to the public. He was also considered in some quarters to be less than entirely open in his Turf operations: his trainer Tom Coulthwaite had had his licence withdrawn earlier in 1913 over the running of two Ismay horses, though this was widely held to be an injustice. Whether personal acrimony stimulated Loder can only be surmise, but it is certainly likely that Bill Saxby, jocked off Craganour after the Two Thousand Guineas, would not be bending over backwards to support that horse's cause in the enquiry in which, as rider of Louvois, he was called to give evidence.

Whatever the validity of such speculation, the amended result stood, for Ismay's appeal the following weekend came too late. That it did stand is just as well for the connections of Aboyeur, who were reported to have won £40,000 in bets on the horse. He ran twice more, beaten on both occasions, and was then sold to the Imperial Racing Club of St Petersburg for £13,000. Craganour never ran again in England and was exported to Argentina, where he enjoyed great success as a sire.

Herbert Jones, Anmer's rider, was not seriously injured. While recovering in hospital he received a thoughtful telegram from Queen Mary, who expressed herself 'very sorry indeed to hear of your sad accident caused through the abominable behaviour of a brutal, lunatic woman'.

The woman herself lay in Epsom Cottage Hospital for four days without regaining consciousness. Her friends and supporters showered her with mail. So did some less sympathetic correspondents: 'I am glad to hear that you are in hospital. I hope you suffer torture until you die. You idiot. I consider you are a person unworthy of existence in this world, considering what you have done. I should like the opportunity of starving and beating you to a pulp. Why don't your people find an asylum for you? Yours etc., An Englishman.' She died on Sunday 8 June. A fractured skull and haemorrhaging of the brain were the causes of death, and after the official inquest the Coroner at Epsom recorded a verdict of death by misadventure.

Five years after Emily Davison's death the first women won the vote.

*Desert Orchid is out of the picture as Norton's Coin (left) and Toby Tobias fly the last fence.*

❮ *More of a candidate for last place than first* ❯

Sirrell Griffiths got out of bed at 3.45 a.m. on his dairy farm just outside the village of Nantgaredig, near Carmarthen in South Wales. He had a busy day ahead of him, and although he did not yet know it, he would not be able to get back to bed until nearly twenty-four hours later.

Having milked his seventy-five Friesian cows, he set about the main business of the day, loading Norton's Coin, one of only three horses he trained under permit on his farm, into the horsebox, then taking the wheel to drive his stable star to Cheltenham. For this was Gold Cup day, and Norton's Coin had a very small supporting role in a performance that Thursday afternoon which would see the hugely popular grey Desert Orchid set off fresh waves of fanaticism with a second victory in the most coveted prize of the National Hunt season. Norton's Coin's participation in the race was something of a mistake, for Sirrell Griffiths had wanted to run him in the Cathcart Challenge Cup on the same day of the Cheltenham meeting, only to discover that the horse was ineligible. By then it was too late to enter him for his other preferred Cheltenham Festival target, the Mildmay of Flete Handicap Chase, so he had to take his chance in the big one.

Although he had not a prayer against Desert Orchid in the Gold Cup, Norton's Coin

came to Cheltenham with the reputation of being a useful enough horse despite lowly origins. Griffiths had bought his sire Mount Cassino for 700 guineas in 1975 (mainly to cover cobs and ponies) and had put the stallion to the unraced Thoroughbred mare Grove Chance, whom he had purchased for just £425. He sold Grove Chance, then in foal for the first time, to his neighbour Percy Thomas, but when she died shortly after giving birth to Norton's Coin he bought back the foal. Norton's Coin won four point-to-points out of ten runs over three seasons and then developed into a good chaser: by the time of his Gold Cup attempt he had won four of his fourteen races under Rules, including a valuable chase at Cheltenham the previous April. Not for him, though, the heated boxes and all-weather gallops of Newmarket or Lambourn. He was housed in a converted milking shed and brought to fitness by being ridden around the farm, when time allowed, by Sirrell Griffiths himself – all fifteen and a half stone of him – and occasionally by the Chief Constable of the Avon and Somerset Police, David Shattock. Lack of peak fitness had told against him on his first run of the 1989–90 season when pitched in against Desert Orchid and other top chasers in the King George VI Rank Chase at Kempton Park on Boxing Day. He caught the eye with a highly encouraging performance despite finishing last but was not seriously considered to be in the same league as the adored 'Dessie'.

Desert Orchid would not have given Norton's Coin a second thought since their Kempton meeting, for he had his public to deal with. His Cheltenham Gold Cup victory in 1989 (see pages 66–9) had unleashed a wave of public adulation unparalleled in racing history. His manure was not sold (as Red Rum's had been), nor had his exploits been celebrated in song (as was the case with Arkle, Red Rum and Dawn Run), but his fans were not sold short: there were books (three), video tapes (two), countless portraits, a white rocking horse called 'Dessie', sculptures and figurines (some of which actually bore a resemblance to the horse), an official fan club, and even a recorded phone message on which Desert Orchid's part-owner Richard Burridge would update

*Norton's Coin gets up to pass
Tody Tobias (right) as Desert
Orchid (left) plugs on to be third.*

**Tote Cheltenham Gold Cup**

Cheltenham
3¼ miles
15 March 1990

1 Norton's Coin  G. McCourt    100–1
2 Toby Tobias   M. Pitman     8–1
3 Desert Orchid  R. Dunwoody   10–11 fav.

*Also ran:* Cavvies Clown (4th), Pegwell Bay,
Maid Of Money, Yahoo, Bonanza Boy,
Kildimo, Ten Of Spades, Nick The Brief, The
Bakewell Boy

12 ran

Winner owned and trained by S. G. Griffiths

*Distances:* ¾ length, 4 lengths

worshippers on the well-being of their idol.

When it was announced that he would be
entered in the Grand National a fierce
debate raged about whether the nation's
best-loved horse should take part in such a
dangerous event: the letters columns of the
sporting press argued the pros and cons for
weeks, a national newspaper ran an opinion
poll (in which the voters came down very
heavily against his participation), and the
publication of the weights for the race (Desert Orchid twelve stone two pounds) added
fuel to the fire. Eventually it was announced
that he would not run – not in 1990, at least
– and the fuss subsided, but Desert Orchid
was clearly more than a national favourite.
He was now a national issue.

'The Grey Horse' had enjoyed a fine season, losing just once (when conceding a
great deal of weight in a handicap over two
miles, a distance now too short for him to
show his best), and winning the King
George VI Rank Chase, steeplechasing's
other classic, for the third time. Less than a
month before the Gold Cup he had produced what for many experts was his best
performance ever when bouncing around
Kempton Park to win the Racing Post Chase
under top weight. He was in good shape and
in good heart, and although it was known
that he did not run up to his best at Chelten-

ham, the conditions would suit him much
more than those of a year ago and few
opposed him. For the adoring public which
flocked to Cheltenham to pay him homage
(the official attendance was 56,884), defeat
was simply out of the question.

Cheltenham Festival racegoers in 1990
enjoyed three days of spring sunshine, and
the going was good to firm – conditions
almost unheard-of on Gold Cup day. On the
first day the Champion Hurdle had been won
by Kribensis (owned by Sheikh Mohammed
and trained by Michael Stoute) from
Nomadic Way (owned by Robert Sangster
and trained by Barry Hills) – powerful Flat
racing connections elbowing in on the
jumping scene. The Gold Cup was to
demonstrate that there was still some room
for the small man.

Desert Orchid faced eleven opponents, of
whom those most likely to spoil the party
were Bonanza Boy (twice winner of the
Welsh National and representative of the
formidable combination of trainer Martin
Pipe and jockey Peter Scudamore), Toby
Tobias (a highly promising young chaser
trained by Jenny Pitman and ridden by her
son Mark), Nick The Brief (who on his last
appearance had easily won the Vincent
O'Brien Irish Gold Cup at Leopardstown)
and Cavvies Clown (trained like Desert
Orchid by David Elsworth and second in the
Gold Cup in 1988). Though ridden by Graham McCourt, then third in the jump jockeys' table, Norton's Coin was a rank outsider.
The *Sporting Life*'s run-down of the runners
described him as 'this no-hoper'; the *Racing
Post* did not mention him at all in its main
preview of the race; and the official Cheltenham racecard form guide nominated him
'more of a candidate for last place than first'.

Described by his owner-trainer as 'a long,
leeky, plain-looking horse', Norton's Coin
ambled along quietly while the fan club
squeaked its excitement at the appearance
of Desert Orchid, striding jauntily around
the parade ring and clearly eager to get on
with the business. Ripples of applause
greeted the great grey as he cantered past
the stands to the start under jockey Richard
Dunwoody, who had taken over as Desert
Orchid's regular partner on the retirement
of Simon Sherwood. Dunwoody had in the

The finishers return to unsaddle. Tom Morgan on Yahoo (yellow colours) leans across Richard Dunwoody on Desert Orchid to congratulate winning jockey Graham McCourt.

Mr and Mrs Sirrell Griffiths with unexpected extra luggage for the journey home.

past won on Norton's Coin and would have been riding him in the Gold Cup had Desert Orchid been absent.

The public was putting its money where its heart was, and at the off Desert Orchid was 11–10 on favourite (though he had opened in the betting at slightly shorter odds). Of the others, only Bonanza Boy (15–2) and Toby Tobias (8–1) started at less than 10–1. Norton's Coin, who had been 200–1 with some bookmakers that morning, started at 100–1 having opened in the course betting at 66–1. Only The Bakewell Boy, a *real* no-hoper, was at longer odds.

As expected Desert Orchid went straight into the lead, and after putting in extravagant leaps at the first two fences seemed to be set fair for an exhibition round. But as the field swung away from the stands for the first time it became clear that the grey would not have matters entirely to his liking, for first Kildimo and then Ten Of Spades kept him close company and would not allow him to dominate affairs. With a circuit to race Nick The Brief was pulled up, and though Desert Orchid continued to dispute the lead with Ten Of Spades as the runners went away from the stands for the second circuit Toby Tobias and Norton's Coin were making noticeable progress through the field. At the fifteenth fence, on the uphill stretch, Kildimo fell and Ten Of Spades went two lengths clear of Desert Orchid. The favourite still seemed to be going well enough, however, and the adoring masses were not particularly worried as the leading group – Ten Of Spades and Desert Orchid, with Toby Tobias and Norton's Coin close behind – thundered down towards the third last fence. The race was really on now, and as the quartet came away from the third last and turned into the straight Desert Orchid suddenly had a fight on his hands – not from Ten Of Spades, who had exhausted himself in drawing the grey's sting and now fell heavily at the second last, but from Toby Tobias and Norton's Coin. The three came to the last fence together,

Desert Orchid on the stands side, Toby Tobias on the far rails, Norton's Coin between them. Desert Orchid had often won from worse positions, but he seemed unable to quicken, and was half a length down on his two younger rivals as they landed over the last obstacle. Toby Tobias was quickest away and Desert Orchid could find no more, but the race was far from finished, for as Mark Pitman on Toby Tobias made for the winning post Graham McCourt urged Norton's Coin to a final effort, and as the two jockeys, whips swishing, pushed their courageous mounts up the hill the cheers from the stands which moments before had been tuning up for another Dessie triumph lapsed into a disbelieving murmur: this was not the right script at all. Desert Orchid was beaten, but ahead of him two brave steeplechasers were fighting out a stirring finish, and fifty yards from the line the no-hoper, the candidate for last place rather than first, stuck his plain-looking chestnut head in front and kept it there. Norton's Coin had won the Cheltenham Gold Cup.

It took a while for the true magnitude of his achievement to dawn on the crowd, shell-shocked as they were by the defeat of their hero. But there was no semblance of a fluke about the result – it was the fastest Gold Cup ever run – and as Norton's Coin made the long walk past the stands to the winner's enclosure he started to receive the reception he deserved. At 100–1 he was the longest-priced winner in the history of the race, but that was not the point. What made the result so glorious was that it epitomized the essence of steeplechasing: at its most prestigious moment the sport had returned to its rural roots and shown that the humblest contestants can win the biggest prizes. Norton's Coin was not the subject of videos and telephone hotlines and fan clubs and exquisitely crafted models and opinion polls. He lived in a converted cowshed and was exercised by his owner, who raced his three horses simply for the fun of it.

Norton's Coin got back to his cowshed at about 10.30 p.m. After the horse was bedded down it was time for Sirrell to celebrate properly, and most of Nantgaredig turned up to assist: he eventually got to bed at 3 a.m. Two hours later he was up again to milk the cows.

# MICHAEL DICKINSON

*Cheltenham Gold Cup*
*Cheltenham, 17 March 1983*

*Bregawn (right) and Captain John jump the last fence, with Silver Buck (red cap) well beaten.*

*Come on, my lot!*

The Cheltenham Gold Cup was won in 1983 by Bregawn from Captain John and Wayward Lad, with Silver Buck fourth and Ashley House fifth. All five were trained by Michael Dickinson.

Dickinson was no stranger to success in the Gold Cup – he had trained the first two home, Silver Buck and Bregawn, in 1982 – but his feat in the 1983 contest is unique in big-race records, and to find anything remotely comparable you have to go back to 1822, when James Croft's four runners in the St Leger filled the first four places. Dickinson had already set a new training record earlier in the 1982–3 season when sending out the winners of twelve races on Boxing Day 1982. The son of Tony and Monica Dickinson, who respectively preceded and succeeded him in charge at Poplar House, Harewood (not far from Leeds in Yorkshire), Michael Dickinson had ridden 378 winners in eleven seasons as as a jockey before taking out a trainer's licence for the 1980–1 season. He trained eighty-four winners that season (including Silver Buck in the King George VI Chase at Kempton Park), and the following season was champion trainer for the first time (with the same number of winners and a strike rate of winners to runners of an astounding 44.9 per cent). But his performance in the 1982–3 campaign was phenomenal, for not only was he producing winners in quantity and at a very high strike rate, he

was also winning big races: before the Gold Cup, Bregawn had won the Hennessy Cognac Gold Cup at Newbury, Silver Buck the Edward Hanmer Memorial Chase at Haydock Park, Captain John the SGB Handicap Chase at Ascot, Wayward Lad the King George VI Chase and Ashley House the Peter Marsh Handicap Chase at Haydock.

With that painstaking attention to detail which is always held to characterize genius, Dickinson had spent the Sunday morning before the Gold Cup briefing his stable jockeys, Robert Earnshaw (Silver Buck), Graham Bradley (Bregawn) and the assistant trainer Dermot Browne (Ashley House), and on the morning of the race walked round the course with these three, Jonjo O'Neill (Wayward Lad) and David Goulding (Captain John) to discuss riding strategy. Of the quintet Bradley looked to have the best chance: second in the Gold Cup in 1982 and a gutsy winner of the Hennessy, the nine-year-old Bregawn was clearly a chaser of great ability, though he had begun to show signs of temperament, being reluctant to line up for the start on occasion. Silver Buck, now eleven, had won four of his five races during the 1982–3 season but had been beaten in the King George by Wayward Lad, who had not run since and whose participation at Cheltenham had been in doubt until a searching gallop had proved his readiness. Only Ashley House had given Dickinson no training problems, but, good chaser as he was, he seemed to be a little out of his depth here.

Six other horses were in the line-up, of which the most fancied were Combs Ditch, who had beaten Bregawn in their warm-up race at Wincanton, Fifty Dollars More, winner of the Mackeson Gold Cup on the course the previous November, and Brown Chamberlin, a promising eight-year-old from Fred Winter's stable who had won the Sun Alliance Chase in 1982. Bregawn started 100–30 favourite, with Combs Ditch second favourite at 9–2. Of the other Dickinson runners, Silver Buck was 5–1, Wayward Lad 6–1, Captain John 11–1 and Ashley House 12–1.

Bregawn gave no trouble at the start and in the early stages of the race stayed close behind the leader, 500–1 outsider Whiggie Geo. Climbing the hill for the first time

*Michael Dickinson with his Famous Five: left to right: Ashley House, Silver Buck, Wayward Lad, Captain John, Bregawn.*

Whiggie Geo dropped back and Bradley decided to try to make the rest of the running. At the end of the first circuit Brown Chamberlin, who had been jumping sketchily, was pulled up, and as the field came past the stands and swung away into the country again Bregawn kept up his gallop. Towards the top of the hill he made two bad jumping errors but these made little difference to his progress, and with Fifty Dollars More falling at the final open ditch only Combs Ditch looked to have any chance of getting in the way of a Dickinson clean sweep.

'Come on, my lot!' The trainer, watching the race on a television screen in the weighing room, had gazed in silence until the field reached the top of the hill and turned towards the stands for the last time. Now he shouted his encouragement, and come on his lot did. Bregawn swept over the third fence from home and made his way into the straight, pursued by Captain John (who had lost ground when blundering at the third last), Wayward Lad and Silver Buck. By the second last only Captain John looked dangerous, and at the final fence Bregawn had it sewn up, scampering up the hill to win by five lengths. Wayward Lad was one and a half lengths further away in third, Silver Buck a tired and remote fourth, and then Ashley House stayed on up the hill to pass Combs Ditch amid cheering never before heard for a horse running fifth!

In recognition of this surely unrepeatable feat the Stewards allowed Ashley House to join his four stable companions in the unsaddling enclosure, and he it was who first received the attentions of his trainer. In post-race interviews Dickinson emphasized the difficulties of getting a horse fit and ready for the Gold Cup, let alone winning it, and he confided that the stress and tension of training the five had caused him to lose a stone in weight since Christmas. But Bregawn was

the winner, and the £45,260 he earned that afternoon made a major contribution to the £358,837 prize money which saw Michael Dickinson champion trainer again that season, with 120 winners in all – a record total – from 259 runners, a strike rate just short of one in two. (His record stood only until the 1988–9 season, when Martin Pipe trained the winners of 208 races, but at a lower strike rate of 37 per cent.)

The next phase of Dickinson's career was not a happy one. After winning a third trainer's title in the 1983–84 season he left Yorkshire and took over as private trainer to Robert Sangster at Manton. He transformed the famous estate into one of the most modern training complexes in the world, but in November 1986 it was announced that Sangster and Dickinson were to part company, and the trainer took his skills to the USA.

Bregawn's temperament got the better of him the following season, and on his racecourse appearances he displayed increasing sourness. He was fitted in blinkers for the 1984 Gold Cup but behaved mulishly, twice trying to pull himself up before finishing a distant sixth to Burrough Hill Lad. Thereafter his behaviour deteriorated further. Trained in Ireland at the Cullinane yard for his first run of the 1984–5 season, he was then moved to Paddy Mullins, winning a handicap hurdle at Limerick Junction on his second outing for his new stable before his mood let him down again in the 1985 Gold Cup: he tried to pull himself up after a circuit and was tailed off when refusing at the last fence.

But the memory of Bregawn should not be of a recalcitrant mule goaded into action as the rest of the field leaves him way behind, but of a good Cheltenham Gold Cup winner storming up the hill to head the procession of Dickinson horses which was the most remarkable training feat of modern times.

## Tote Cheltenham Gold Cup

Cheltenham
3¼ miles
17 March 1983

| 1 | Bregawn | G. Bradley | 100–30 fav. |
| 2 | Captain John | D. Goulding | 11–1 |
| 3 | Wayward Lad | J. J. O'Neill | 6–1 |

*Also ran:* Silver Buck (4th), Ashley House, Richdee, Midnight Love, Combs Ditch, Fifty Dollars More, Whiggie Geo, Brown Chamberlin

11 ran

Winner owned by J. Kennelly, trained by M. Dickinson

*Distances:* 5 lengths, 1½ lengths

# DAWN RUN

*Cheltenham Gold Cup*
*Cheltenham, 13 March 1986*

*The triumphant return.*

Statues of three famous horses preside over the Cheltenham parade ring. From his vantage point high in the new stand Golden Miller, five times winner of the Gold Cup, pricks his ears. At the top end of the paddock Arkle haughtily stares into the distance. And at the point where the placed horses enter the paddock to unsaddle after the race stands a bronze of the mare Dawn Run, with jockey Jonjo O'Neill patting her neck.

It is entirely fitting that Dawn Run should share the statuary honours with the other two Cheltenham legends, for she was the first – and to date the only – horse to win both the Champion Hurdle and the Cheltenham Gold Cup. And it is especially fitting that her statue should stand so close to the

parade ring, the scene of such joyous pandemonium at Cheltenham after she had completed her unique double in March 1986.

Dawn Run, trained in Ireland by Paddy Mullins, was favourite for the 1986 Gold Cup. A tall, well-built mare, she first encroached on the English racing scene in spring 1983: she came second to Sabin Du Loir in the Sun Alliance Hurdle at the Cheltenham Festival; three weeks later, ridden by her trainer's son Tony, she ran on successive days at Liverpool, winning on the Friday and the next day running Gaye Brief, fresh from his Champion Hurdle success, to a length. The following Christmas she beat Gaye Brief by a neck in a thrilling race at Kempton Park and three months later (in the meantime winning the Wessel Cable Champion Hurdle

*Dawn Run is third behind Wayward Lad and Forgive 'N Forget at the final fence.*

Cheltenham Gold Cup was her target, and in January 1986 Dawn Run was sent over to Cheltenham to run in the Holsten Distributors Chase as a preliminary to her big date less than two months later. Tony Mullins was again in the saddle, but the reconnaissance mission was a disaster. Never the most fluent of jumpers, she put in some unncessarily extravagant leaps before settling down on the second circuit, but then met the final open ditch all wrong and deposited the hapless Mullins on the floor. He remounted immediately and set off in pursuit of the other runners, but as a Gold Cup trial the race was a mess, and the announcement that Jonjo O'Neill was once more to replace Mullins for the big race came as no surprise.

So Dawn Run came to Cheltenham on Gold Cup day with only four races over fences behind her, and in many quarters it was felt that inexperience would prove her downfall against her much more seasoned rivals. Ten lined up against her, including the first three in the previous year's race – Forgive 'N Forget, Righthand Man and Earls Brig. On Forgive 'N Forget's most recent outing he had run fourth behind Combs Ditch at Haydock Park, and that horse was also in the Gold Cup field, third favourite after a highly successful season which had brought him three good prizes and a neck defeat by Wayward Lad in the King George VI Chase at Kempton Park. That was Wayward Lad's third victory in the King George, and now he was making his fourth attempt to win the Gold Cup. Another runner to attract support was Run And Skip, who had won four races that season – including the Coral Welsh National at Chepstow – and come second in the Hennessy Cognac Gold Cup.

These were old hands, and Dawn Run was effectively still a novice. She faced a stiff task but started at 15–8 to overcome her inexperience in – very significantly – the first Gold Cup to give mares a five-pound weight concession. Forgive 'N Forget started at 7–2, with Combs Ditch 9–2, Run And Skip 15–2 and Wayward Lad 8–1.

Dawn Run took the lead from the start and hopped nimbly over the first two fences. But as the runners made round the left-hand bend in front of the stands and set off into the

at Leopardstown) took advantage of his absence from the Champion Hurdle line-up to become the first mare to win the race since African Sister in 1939, though she had to fight hard before scrambling home by three quarters of a length from Cima. Her jockey at Cheltenham was twice-champion Jonjo O'Neill, brought in earlier in the season to replace Tony Mullins. Dawn Run then won the Sandeman Hurdle at Liverpool and the Prix la Barka at Auteuil as a prelude to her victory in the Grande Course de Haies d'Auteuil, the French equivalent of the Champion Hurdle. By mid-1984 Dawn Run had won the Champion Hurdle in three countries.

Her first run over fences was on 1 November 1984, in the Nobber Chase at Navan. She duly won, but was then sidelined by a leg injury and did not appear again until December 1985, when she won chases at Punchestown and Leopardstown. By now the country for the first time she was joined in the lead by Run And Skip, and the company clearly put her off, for she hit the third fence hard. For the rest of the first circuit Run And Skip and Dawn Run, both regular front-runners, vied for the lead on the fast ground, and their duel took them well clear of the rest of the field. At the water jump on the second circuit – the fourteenth of the twenty-two fences – the mare dropped her hind legs in the water, and this mistake handed the initiative to Run And Skip. But Dawn Run was back alongside by the next fence only to suffer another reverse when clouting the fifth from home. Now the heat was being turned on, and this was where her inexperience would really tell. At the top of the hill she was still in the forefront of matters with Run And Skip, but behind them Wayward Lad and Forgive 'N Forget were travelling smoothly and coming ever closer. Righthand Man was not far in arrears but started to lose ground as the principal four swept down the hill. At the third last Run And Skip touched down just in front of the mare, who was soon under pressure. But Dawn Run was not a horse to give in meekly, and as the four came round into the straight she stuck resolutely to her guns. At the second last she put in a tremendous leap and was back in the lead as Run And Skip started to fade, but Forgive 'N Forget on the stands side and Wayward Lad inside him were now going for home, and they passed Dawn Run on the approach to the last. Here Forgive 'N Forget made a mistake and handed the initiative to Wayward Lad, but he was very tired and started to wander to the left towards the rails. To Jonjo O'Neill, who a moment earlier had been plugging on towards a certain third place, this sign of weakness in Wayward Lad's finishing effort offered remote but renewed hope: 'I suddenly saw he was tiring,' he reported later, 'and so did she.' The jockey managed to spur Dawn Run to one last effort, switching her from the inside to rally up the centre of the course. With great courage she fought her way past Forgive 'N Forget, but halfway up the run-in Wayward Lad was still two lengths up. He was out on his feet, though, and when Dawn Run appeared on his right he had no answer. A few yards before the winning post she found

yet more courage and stamina and forced herself in front to win by a length.

This was real racing history being made – and, what's more, being made by an Irish mare ridden by the most popular Irish-born jockey around at the Cheltenham National Hunt Festival, Ireland's annual pilgrimage to English racing. The crowd in the stands had been roused to fever pitch by the drama of the finish and the almost unbelievable manner in which Dawn Run had come through to win, and now complete mayhem broke out. Hats were flung into the air, the cheering reached higher and higher levels, and Dawn Run and Jonjo O'Neill were engulfed as they came back past the stands and up the walkway to the unsaddling enclosure in the parade ring. It was hardly a stately progress, but as she made her triumphant way back the seas of people around her grew and grew, so that she was accompanied back into the parade ring by a whooping mob, pushing and shoving to get to her, all carried along on a tide of exultation. Nor did the tide ebb once the horse was unsaddled: Jonjo O'Neill, having weighed in, hoisted the rejected Tony Mullins on to his shoulders, and the diminutive Mrs Hill was lifted into the air by the ecstatic mob. There has never been anything like it at Cheltenham.

All this jubilation had a sad epilogue. On her next outing Dawn Run came down at the very first fence at Liverpool, giving Jonjo O'Neill a terrible fall. Worse was to follow for the great mare, for after winning a match at Punchestown against Buck House (who the day before her Gold Cup victory had won the two-mile Queen Mother Champion Chase at Cheltenham) and running second in the Prix la Barka at Auteuil, she returned to the French course in June to attempt a repeat victory in the Grand Course de Haies. This time tragedy struck: at the fifth last obstacle she fell and broke her neck, dying instantly.

Steeplechasing can exact a terrible price from its participants, but it can also provide moments of unparalleled sporting rapture. No one who saw the 1986 Gold Cup and knew of Dawn Run's subsequent fate could look with unmixed emotions on her statue by the Cheltenham parade ring, where she left a permanent mark on racing history.

## Tote Cheltenham Gold Cup

Cheltenham
3¼ miles
13 March 1986

| 1 Dawn Run | J. J. O'Neill | 15–8 fav. |
| 2 Wayward Lad | G. Bradley | 8–1 |
| 3 Forgive 'N Forget | M. Dwyer | 7–2 |

*Also ran:* Run And Skip (4th), Righthand Man, Observe, Earls Brig, Von Trappe, Combs Ditch, Castle Andrea, Cybrandian

11 ran

Winner owned by Mrs C. D. Hill, trained by P. Mullins

*Distances:* 1 length, 2½ lengths

# PRETTY POLLY

*Gold Cup*
*Ascot, 21 June 1906*

*❞ Alas, and again Alas! Pretty Polly beaten! ❞*

Many of the races described in this book produced famous victories. The 1906 Ascot Gold Cup produced a famous defeat.

Pretty Polly was indisputably one of the outstanding racemares of all time. Owned and bred in Ireland by Major Eustace Loder (she was foaled only two years after Sceptre (see pages 18–19)) and trained at Newmarket by Peter Purcell Gilpin, she made her racecourse debut in the British Dominion Two-Year-Old Plate at Sandown Park in June 1903 and turned in an electrifying performance to win by an official margin of ten lengths – though some put the correct distance at nearly a hundred yards! That Pretty Polly was something out of the ordinary was confirmed as she sailed unbeaten through a nine-race campaign as a two-year-old and continued to carry all before her in 1904, notching up facile victories in the One Thousand Guineas (at 4–1 on), the Oaks (100–8 on), the Coronation Stakes (5–1 on), the Nassau Stakes (33–1 on), the St Leger (5–2 on) and – just two days after the final Classic – the Park Hill Stakes (25–1 on). In October this seemingly unbeatable filly went to France for the Prix du Conseil Municipal, and here she met her first defeat, beaten two and a half lengths by the 66–1 outsider Presto. There were plenty of excuses (she had endured a very bad journey to Paris, the going was appallingly heavy, and her regular jockey William Lane was injured and could not take the ride), and she resumed her winning ways later that month with an easy stroll in the Free Handicap at Newmarket. As a four-year-old she won all her four races, including the Coronation Cup, the Champion Stakes and the Jockey Club Cup; in her other race she started at 55–1 on to defeat a solitary opponent. She was kept in training as a five-year-old with her main target the Ascot Gold Cup, and arrived at the Royal meeting unbeaten in her two earlier races that season: never much of a betting proposition once her ability became apparent, Pretty Polly started at 1000–35 on in the March Stakes at Newmarket and at 11–2 on in the Coronation Cup at Epsom (despite the presence in the latter of the 1904 Derby winner St Amant). She sauntered through both.

And so to Ascot, where she started at 11–4 on to beat just four opponents for the two-and-a-half-mile marathon. She had only once before raced at a distance beyond two miles, in the Jockey Club Cup at Newmarket in November 1905, when she had won, hard held, by half a length from Bachelor's Button. Now seven years old, Bachelor's Button was to take Pretty Polly on again, and started 7–1 joint second favourite with the 1905 Derby winner Cicero. Bachelor's Button was not of Classic calibre but had won many good races, including the Champion Stakes in 1904 and the Hardwicke Stakes and Doncaster Cup in 1905. He came to Ascot fresh from a victory under nine stone in the Manchester Cup, and would have the benefit of a pacemaker, St Denis – who had himself won the Princess of Wales's Stakes and run third to St Amant in the 1904 Derby. The three-year-old Achilles completed the field.

Pretty Polly's jockey in the Gold Cup was Bernard Dillon: he had ridden her several times before. But so had Danny Maher, who now had the ride on Bachelor's Button, and who was of the opinion that Pretty Polly did not have sufficient reserves to last home in the Gold Cup. His ride against her when beaten half a length on Bachelor's Button in the previous season's Jockey Club Cup had convinced him that her stamina was flawed. By now Pretty Polly was a national heroine, and to the vast throng which crowded into Ascot any suggestion of defeat was heresy. But already there had been hints that this would not be her day. When she had won the Coronation Cup a wart was beginning to grow on her belly, and this had been lanced not long before the Gold Cup. There were even rumours that her condition would force her withdrawal, but such scares proved unfounded and she duly arrived in the paddock. Fresh doubts were raised here: the mare was bathed in sweat and seemed uncharacteristically agitated and disinclined for the job in hand. It was clear to the crush of admirers which pressed around her that she was not at her best.

St Denis, the 500–1 outsider (despite his Classic form) on account of his role as pacemaker for Bachelor's Button, went straight about his task and took a good lead as the runners came past the stands, packed with

*Bachelor's Button throws the racing world into mourning by beating Pretty Polly.*

*Pretty Polly attracts admiration in the paddock.*

**Gold Cup**

Ascot
2½ miles
21 June 1906

| 1 Bachelor's Button | D. Maher | 7–1 |
| 2 Pretty Polly | B. Dillon | 4–11 fav. |
| 3 Achilles | A. Templeman | 40–1 |

*Also ran:* Cicero (4th), St Denis

5 ran

Winner owned by S. B. Joel, trained by C. Peck

*Distances:* 1 length, 5 lengths

morning-dressed spectators on a stiflingly hot afternoon. Achilles was second, with Cicero, reluctant to settle, third. Bachelor's Button and Pretty Polly brought up the rear. The pacemaker maintained a good gallop as the runners swept away from the stands down towards Swinley Bottom and still had the lead as they made the long right-hand turn with just under a mile to go. From here to the final stages it was all uphill, and with six furlongs left St Denis had had enough, so Achilles took up the running until the runners came into the straight. Cicero, whose stamina had been in doubt, could not keep his place and dropped away, but Bachelor's Button and Pretty Polly – the mare on the stands side, her rival on the far side – were closing rapidly on the leader. Achilles tired and veered towards the stands, seeming to some spectators to carry Pretty Polly wide, but once past she appeared to be set for victory. Maher on Bachelor's Button, however, was still convinced that his mount could outstay her and held on tenaciously. A hundred yards out Dillon drew his whip and Pretty Polly was hit for the first time in her racing career, but it was no good. Bachelor's Button was the stronger, and went on to win by a length.

The crowd was stunned, and Bachelor's Button returned to unsaddle in almost complete silence. For once the cliche that racegoers wept openly was all too true, but these were tears of real sadness – though it was hardly fair to 'blame' her conqueror, who had won the race in dour style (and afterwards took the Jockey Club Cup from his sole opponent Achilles before ending his racing career unplaced in the Prix du Conseil Municipal). The notion that Pretty Polly was simply beaten by a better horse at the distance on the day was well down the list of possible explanations for her defeat, and George Lambton aired the widely held view that jockeyship had proved the decisive factor: Bachelor's Button 'was a sterling good horse, especially at Ascot, but he was not a Persimmon, and if a real good jockey had been on Pretty Polly I think she might just have scrambled home.' Trainer Gilpin echoed that view when claiming after the race that Dillon had disobeyed his instructions – 'No doubt he was carried away by the excitement.' Add the possible problem with the wart, her upset at being all but mobbed by the crowd on a very hot day, and her apparently being carried off a true course in the straight by Achilles, and you have a long menu of excuses or explanations. In all probability it was a combination of several factors, not least the suspected flaw in her stamina which made her vulnerable once that fierce early pace had been set by St Denis.

Whatever the reason, the gloom which her defeat threw over the racing scene was genuine. The *Sporting Life* the following day paid no lip-service to impartial journalism: 'Alas, and again Alas! Pretty Polly beaten! Lamentations as sincere as they were loud were heard on every hand after the race was over.' Sadly she had no chance to make amends, for she suffered a setback in training when being prepared for the Doncaster Cup and was retired. Rarely has the Turf seen her like.

# GORDON RICHARDS AND PINZA

*Derby Stakes*
*Epsom, 6 June 1953*

*The newly crowned Queen and the newly knighted jockey meet on the way to the parade ring.*

❜ *My mind was in a turmoil, and my brain perhaps a little numbed* ❜

Few races have ever produced such a division of loyalties as the Derby in 1953. This was Coronation year, and the young Queen Elizabeth II, crowned in Westminster Abbey just four days before the running of the race, had a real chance of owning the winner in Aureole. Among his opponents was Pinza, ridden by Gordon Richards, the most successful and (more to the point) most loved jockey in British Turf

history, yet still trying to win the Derby after twenty-seven unavailing attempts: to add further spice to the occasion, the announcement had just been made that Richards had been awarded a knighthood, the first jockey to be so honoured. Victory for either horse would be received rapturously, but at the same time with a tinge of disappointment.

Oblivious to the emotion riding on their backs, Aureole and Pinza came to Epsom with excellent credentials. Aureole, trained by Captain Cecil Boyd-Rochfort and ridden by Harry Carr, had scored a smooth victory in the Lingfield Derby Trial. Pinza was owned by Sir Victor Sassoon (who had spent a huge amount of money over many years trying to win the Derby) and trained by Norman Bertie. He had won the Dewhurst Stakes by six lengths as a two-year-old but had been a 33–1 chance for the Derby in the spring of 1953 until an impressive victory in the Newmarket Stakes brought his odds

*Pinza strides home from Aureole.*

*Sir Victor Sassoon leads in his – and Gordon Richards's – first Derby winner.*

**Derby Stakes**

Epsom
1¹/₂ miles
6 June 1953

| 1 | Pinza | G. Richards | 5–1 jt fav. |
| 2 | Aureole | W. H. Carr | 9–1 |
| 3 | Pink Horse | W. R. Johnstone | 33–1 |

*Also ran:* Shikampur (4th), Chatsworth, Pharel, Timberland, Prince Canarina, Nearula, Good Brandy, Mountain King, Windy, Fellermelad, Empire Honey, Prince Charlemagne, Novarullah, Durham Castle, Jaffa, Gala Performance, Fe Shaing, Scipio, Victory Roll, Peter-So-Gay, Star of the Forest, Premonition, City Scandal, Barrowby Court

27 ran

Winner owned by Sir V. Sassoon, trained by N. Bertie

*Distances:* 4 lengths, 1¹/₂ lengths

down to 8–1. Two niggling reservations lingered about Pinza as a Derby horse: his physique – a big horse, he might not be nimble enough down Tattenham Hill – and his temperament, for he was so highly strung that he was invariably ridden by a stable lad when led around the paddock, and the drawn-out preliminaries of the Derby might cause him to boil over. The Queen's Aureole was if anything even more highly strung than Pinza.

In the event both were very much on their toes before the race but behaved well enough. Pinza started 5–1 joint favourite with Premonition, who had won at Epsom and York earlier in the season. Aureole, despite attracting all that monarchist money, was a 9–1 shot, with the Two Thousand Guineas winner Nearula at 10–1. In all, twenty-seven runners went to post, but this Derby's appearance of being an extremely open race was not to last long.

The early running was made by the 100–1 outsider City Scandal, who after two fur-

longs conceded the lead to Shikampur, with Pinza in about sixth place and Aureole unable to take up a handy position. At the top of the hill, about six furlongs out, Shikampur still led while Aureole had made significant improvement, but Gordon Richards had found a welcome opening on the rails on the run down to Tattenham Corner and slipped a perfectly balanced Pinza into second place on the turn for home. Shikampur kept his advantage as Richards roused his mount to full steam, and a quarter of a mile out Pinza swept past and went into a decisive lead. Meanwhile Aureole had got into top gear and came through into second place, but try as he might he could never pose a threat to Pinza, who galloped on relentlessly to win by four lengths, with Pink Horse running on to take third place a length and a half further adrift and the gallant Shikampur a tired fourth.

Ecstatic scenes greeted Gordon Richards as Pinza was led to the unsaddling enclosure, and although to some he seemed oddly unmoved, he wrote subsequently that 'my mind was in a turmoil, and my brain perhaps a little numbed … the reception which the crowd gave me was something out of this world.'

Pinza ran only once more, Gordon Richards partnering him to an easy victory in the King George VI and Queen Elizabeth Stakes at Ascot; Aureole was again second. The intention then was to run Pinza in the St Leger and the Prix de l'Arc de Triomphe, but he broke down and was retired to stud. He was a brilliant horse, and his absence from the top races was keenly felt, though Aureole was the beneficiary as a four-year-old, winning the Coronation Cup, the Hardwicke Stakes and the King George. Premonition, who had never been seen with any chance in the Derby, won the 1953 St Leger. Sadly, the 1954 season saw Richards forced to retire from the saddle by injury; so the 1953 Derby was his last ride in the race as well as his first victory in it.

Sir Victor Sassoon, who had waited so long to own a Derby winner, won three of the next seven runnings. But the 1953 Derby belonged to Gordon Richards. None of his 4,870 victories was more popular than that of Pinza in the 1953 Derby.

# FRED WINTER AND MANDARIN

*Grand Steeplechase de Paris*
*Auteuil, 17 June 1962*

*Bit dangling under his neck, Mandarin holds off Lumino.*

*❝ I couldn't steer him, I couldn't stop, and I was much too frightened to jump off! ❞*

Mandarin was one of the best and toughest British-trained steeplechasers since the War. Fred Winter was one of the most skilful and durable jump jockeys of the same period. What they performed together in Paris in June 1962 almost defied belief.

Mandarin was eleven but showed no signs of losing the powers which had brought him numerous victories, including two in the King George VI Chase. After his second King George, in 1959, he had developed tendon trouble and was given nearly a year's rest by trainer Fulke Walwyn, but if anything he was improving with age, and he had gone

through the 1961–2 season unbeaten. After winning a small chase at Ludlow he took the Hennessy Gold Cup for the second time – highly appropriately, as he was owned by Madame Kilian Hennessy of the sponsoring brandy company – and then, after a warm-up victory at Kempton Park, had beaten Fortria by a length in the Cheltenham Gold Cup. That hard-fought win might have been deemed enough for the season, but his French owner was keen to run her little battler (bred in France) in the top French jumping event – in which he had finished second three years earlier – and so three months after the Gold Cup, when he might have

ABOVE *In retirement at Lambourn, Mandarin reflects with Fred Winter on their afternoon in Paris.*

RIGHT *Mandarin comes back to a hero's welcome.*

thought himself to have earned a summer holiday, Mandarin was despatched to Paris.

The steeplechase course at Auteuil is a far cry from Newbury or Cheltenham, and the runners in the four-mile Grand Steeplechase have to negotiate a bewildering variety of obstacles: some of the fences are soft privet, to be jumped through rather than over; there are two natural brooks, including the Rivière de la Tribune – four metres of water preceded by a hedge one metre high and one metre wide; and then there is Le Bull-finch, a rail, ditch and fence on top of a stone wall. To compound the difficulties, the track itself is a figure-of-eight, with a dizzying number of twists and turns. Mandarin's jockey Fred Winter, four times champion, was no stranger to Auteuil yet still had to work hard at memorizing the peculiar con-figurations of the course. This time his pow-ers of concentration were not helped by the fact that on a hot and humid Sunday after-noon in the Bois de Boulogne he was feeling awful: he had been wasting in order to ride Beaver II at nine stone ten pounds later in the afternoon, and was severely debilitated by a stomach upset which had kept him up all night. Winter then suffered an attack of cramp in the jockeys' changing room and

had to be assisted in preparing for the ride on Mandarin. He claimed to be feeling like 'a bit of chewed-up string' when he walked out for what was to be the finest ride of his life.

Mandarin, a somewhat clumsy horse and a hard puller, was wearing as usual his special bridle which incorporated a rubber-covered bit. As he led the field towards the fourth of the twenty-one fences – a privet hedge nearly six feet high – the bit snapped in two and fell out of Mandarin's mouth, leaving Winter with over three miles to cover and no means of control, the reins dangling use-lessly in his hands. 'What could I do?', he said afterwards: 'I couldn't steer him, I couldn't stop, and I was much too frightened to jump off!' Fortune owed Fred Winter a big favour and provided it, for the next part of this tor-tuous course was quite straight, with four fences to be jumped, and this at least gave the jockey time to work out how to respond to the calamity. Also in his favour was the demeanour of his mount, for although Man-darin must have felt horribly unbalanced he made no attempt to take advantage of this unwonted freedom and run away. Winter discovered that he could apply a limited amount of control by squeezing Mandarin with his knees, by swinging his body to one side or the other, and by applying such pressure as he could with the reins on the horse's neck. He also had the assistance of his rivals, for at the next bend the French jockey Jean Daumas, well aware of the difficulties Winter was in, pushed his mount Taillefer up on Mandarin's outside, and his presence helped keep the British-trained horse on course. But hurtling towards Winter was the most difficult part of the track, where the course divides into three, and the approach to this junction was not railed. Winter had to aim Mandarin for the middle course but his mount started wandering off to the left before pressure from the vice-like grip of the jockey's thighs pointed him in the right direction. Thereafter the company of the other horses kept him on course, and a bad mistake at the water jump on the second circuit worked to Mandarin's advantage, as it put him back to fifth place and gave him horses to follow.

Then, just before the final turn and with four fences to take, it looked as if Mandarin might yet run out, and Winter had to put all his strength into forcing the horse to the left, the correct side of the course marker. This manoeuvre succeeded, but at some cost. Mandarin lost several lengths and – much worse – he had broken down in the tendons of one of his forelegs. Now the runners were nearly into the straight, and Mandarin – lame and exhausted – called up extraordinary reserves of courage to retrieve the forfeited ground. Round the final bend he was still several lengths down but was beginning to claw back the deficit, and at 'Le Bullfinch', two fences out, he was second. At the last he was in front, but he was dead tired and Winter could do nothing to hold him together for the final desperate few yards to the line. Mandarin, head down and drained of all energy, was all out, and it still seemed that his heroic effort might come to nothing, for the French horse Lumino was gaining with every stride and closing inexorably on the leader. At the line no one really knew which had prevailed. As the horses were led back to unsaddle, the broken bit dangling under Mandarin's bowed neck, the result was announced: Mandarin, by a head.

Forty minutes later Fred Winter was again being led in on the winner, for his wasting to ride Beaver II had paid off. But Mandarin never ran again. In his retirement in Lambourn he was the daily recipient of two bottles of Mackeson stout, delivered from the local pub courtesy of Colonel Bill Whitbread, whose company sponsors the Whitbread Gold Cup in which Mandarin was twice runner-up.

John Lawrence (now Lord Oaksey), reporting in the following day's *Daily Telegraph*, afforded this almost unbelievable race an appropriate encomium:

*I never expect to be more moved by a man and a horse than I was by Winter and Mandarin this afternoon. Separately, they have always been superb. Together, to-day, taking disaster by the throat and turning it into victory, they have surely earned a place of honour that will be secure as long as men talk, or read, or think of horses.*

**Grand Steeplechase de Paris**

Auteuil
6500 metres
17 June 1962

| 1 Mandarin | F. Winter | 2–1 fav. |
| 2 Lumino | R. Kirchhofer | 6–1 |
| 3 Paradou | T. Nador | 5–2 |

*Also ran:* Missouri (4th), Pen Hir, Tandour, Taillefer, Indian, Rubis Rose, Pif Paf, Zephyr, Erminette, Portico, Dragon Vert

14 ran

Winner owned by Mme K. Hennessy, trained by F. Walwyn

*Distances:* head, 2 lengths

# BOB CHAMPION AND ALDANITI

*Aldaniti at Becher's Brook on the
second circuit.*

Bob Champion was thirty-one when in the summer of 1979 he was told he had cancer. One of Britain's top jump jockeys, he had ridden the winners of over 350 races in his career and was recognized as one of the toughest of a tough breed. Now he faced the biggest obstacle he would ever have to clear, for the only chance of cure lay in a long and horrifically painful course of chemotherapy. The alternative was death within as little as eight months.

After two courses of treatment, he was driven home to Wiltshire, where he would remain until the start of the third course. Here he was telephoned regularly by trainer Josh Gifford, for whom he had been first jockey before his illness and who had assured him that his position as stable jockey would be waiting for him as soon as he had recovered. The horse of which Bob Champion especially wanted news was Aldaniti.

In 1979 Aldaniti was nine years old, a tall, tough, old-fashioned sort of steeplechaser who had been bought by Josh Gifford at the Ascot sales in May 1974. Aldaniti was back at Ascot for his first race – over hurdles – in

January 1975 and, ridden by Bob Champion, won easily. He was then sold to shipbroker Nick Embiricos, one of Gifford's owners. A bad tendon strain in Aldaniti's off-foreleg had to be fired, and he was on the sidelines for eighteen months. Once back in training he was put over fences: after unseating Champion at Newbury he won at Ascot on 1 April 1977 and was soon being singled out by his connections as a future Grand National winner. Whatever his eventual Liverpool prospects, he was becoming a fine chaser and ran third to Bachelors Hall and Fort Devon in the 1977 Hennessy Cognac Gold Cup at Newbury. But he had chipped two bones in the pastern of his off-hind leg in the race and was sidelined again until fully recovered, remaining in his box from December 1977 until July 1978. The following March Bob Champion rode him into third place behind Alverton in 1979 the Cheltenham Gold Cup (at 40–1) and the month after that Aldaniti ran second to Fighting Fit in the Scottish National at Ayr.

Despite his injury problems Aldaniti was clearly a candidate for the Grand National, and to the stricken Bob Champion the idea

## Grand National

Liverpool
4½ miles
4 April 1981

| 1 Aldaniti | R. Champion | 10–1 |
| 2 Spartan Missile | Mr M. J. Thorne | 8–1 fav. |
| 3 Royal Mail | P. Blacker | 16–1 |

*Also ran:* Three To One (4th), Senator Maclacury, Royal Exile, Rubstic, Coolishall, Rathlek, So, Sebastian V, Cheers, Choral Festival, Martinstown, Might Be, Three Of Diamonds, Pacify, Zongalero, Kylogue Lady, Lord Gulliver, Tenecoon, Carrow Boy, Kininvie, Drumroan, No Gypsy, Another Prospect, Chumson, Kilkilwell, Delmoss, Barney Maclyvie, Another Captain, Royal Stuart, Son And Heir, The Vintner, Deiopea, Dromore, Bryan Boru, Casamayor, My Friendly Cousin

39 ran

Winner owned by S. M. Embiricos, trained by J. T. Gifford

*Distances:* 4 lengths, 2 lengths

*Aldaniti passes the post.*

of winning the Liverpool race on this horse became an inspiration as he awaited his third course of chemotherapy. In the event it took six courses of treatment to eradicate the cancer, and by the time of the 1980 Grand National he was in no condition to take part. But nor was Aldaniti, who had broken down again at Sandown Park in November 1979 and was to spend most of 1980 recuperating at his owner's Sussex home. Meanwhile, Bob Champion had left hospital in January that year. The illness and its treatment had left him bald and so weak that he could hardly stand, but throughout the spring and summer he gradually regained his fitness. His comeback ride – in a flat race at Fairhill, Maryland – was a winning one, and his first competitive ride in Britain since his illness came on Roadhead in a steeplechase at Stratford on 30 August 1980: 'Hail Champion the Wonder Horseman', headlined the *Sporting Life*. Just over three weeks later he won on Physicist at Fontwell Park. Bob Champion was back.

So, eventually, was Aldaniti. In February 1981, after fifteen months *hors de combat*, he made yet another reappearance, this time in the valuable Whitbread Trial Chase at Ascot. Starting at 14–1 and not expected to be fully fit after his long lay-off, he won

easily. Liverpool beckoned, just so long as his legs remained sound.

They did, and on 4 April 1981 Aldaniti started 10–1 second favourite in a field of thirty-nine. Favourite at 8–1 was Spartan Missile, bred, owned, trained and ridden by 54-year-old John Thorne: this brilliant hunter-chaser had twice won the Foxhunters' Chase on the course and was strongly supported to thwart the Champion dream. The 1979 winner Rubstic was on offer at 11–1, followed by 14–1 Zongalero and 16–1 Royal Exile, Royal Stuart and Royal Mail.

Bob Champion had been advised by Fred Winter, who had twice ridden the winner of the Grand National, to take a pull halfway to the first fence in order to prevent his mount from rushing at it. But the horse was not to be restrained:

> *As we came to the fence Aldaniti stood off far too far away, pinged it, but came down much too steep. I slipped my reins to the end of the buckle but I thought we had gone. What a waste for both of us. He was on the ground, down. His nose and knees scraping the grass. We'd had it.*

They hadn't. Aldaniti recovered his balance and sped on towards the second.

> *When he reached it he stood off even further and almost landed on top of it though he never felt like falling. He scraped his belly on it. That hurt him and taught him an even sharper lesson.*

After the third he learned to treat the Liverpool fences with the respect they deserved: from then on his jumping was exemplary, and by the eleventh he had pulled his way into the lead. He turned back towards the stands, jumped nimbly over the thirteenth and fourteenth and soared over the Chair with Sebastian V, Royal Stuart and Zongalero keeping him company and Spartan Missile starting to make ground from the rear. At Becher's Brook on the second circuit he put in a stupendous leap, pitched on landing but was confidently gathered together by Champion to continue on his triumphant way, pursued by Rubstic and Royal Mail. Spartan Missile had made a bad mistake at the eighteenth and Thorne was giving him plenty of time to recover. At the third last Rubstic was back-pedalling and it was still the two crocks – Bob Champion and Aldaniti – making the best of their way home from Royal Mail. As Royal Mail hit the second last hard the fairy-tale result seemed inevitable. Champion let Aldaniti take the last fence in his own time and then set off up the run-in which the jockey later described as 'the loneliest place in the world'. Meanwhile behind him John Thorne was desperately trying to provide some company, for Spartan Missile was running on at a tremendous rate. Third at the last fence, he passed Royal Mail and with just over a furlong to go was finishing so strongly that it looked as if he must catch Aldaniti. Champion picked up his whip and waved it at his mount to encourage him over those last few yards, and Aldaniti responded gamely. He was dead tired but he kept up his gallop, and at the post had four lengths to spare over Spartan Missile, with Royal Mail two lengths further back in third.

The dream had come true. Bob Champion had conquered cancer and Aintree and a horse three times crippled had galloped his rivals into submission. In 1983 the jockey would found the Bob Champion Cancer Trust, and four years later Aldaniti himself (who fell at the first fence in the 1982 National) would play his part in the Trust's fund-raisng activities by undertaking a 250-mile charity walk from London to Liverpool, arriving at the course to massive acclaim on the day of the Grand National: among the riders who partnered the 1981 hero on his trek was the Princess Royal. But Bob Champion's immediate duties after his victory included the obligatory press conference, and his words there sum up why the 1981 Grand National has gone down in history not only as one of the most emotional races ever run, but as perhaps the most inspirational:

*I rode this race for all the patients in hospital. And all the people who look after them. My only wish is that my winning shows them that there is always hope, and all battles can be won.*

*Owner Nick Embiricos (left) greets Aldaniti and Bob Champion in the unsaddling enclosure.*

# LESTER PIGGOTT AND
# COMMANCHE RUN

*Lester Piggott and Commanche
Run leaving the paddock.*

❧ *There's only one St
Leger and there's only one
Lester* ❧

No jockey in British racing history has ridden more Classic winners than Lester Piggott, who notched up twenty-nine triumphs during a riding career which spanned nearly four decades. His first Classic victory came on Never Say Die in the 1954 Derby, his last on Shadeed, who beat Bairn by a head in the 1985 Two Thousand Guineas. Commanche Run's neck victory over Baynoun in the 1984 St Leger gave Piggott his twenty-eighth Classic, breaking the record previously held by Frank Buckle with twenty-seven wins between 1792 and 1827.

The 1984 St Leger was classic Piggott in more ways than one, for the run-up to the race had been accompanied by a typical controversy over whether he had filched the big-race ride from a fellow jockey. Commanche Run was trained at Newmarket by Luca Cumani, whose stable jockey was the American Darrel McHargue. Piggott had replaced McHargue, then sitting out a suspension, on Commanche Run in the Gordon Stakes at Goodwood, which he won by a very wide margin; and though the stable jockey was back on board for the colt's victory in the March Stakes on the same course, his preparation race for the St Leger, Commanche Run's owner Ivan Allan, claiming 'There's only one St Leger and only one Lester,' insisted that his close friend Piggott replace McHargue for the Classic.

Despite a scare with grazed knees during the week before the St Leger, Commanche Run was favourite for the race, and with much justification. He had been lightly campaigned as a two-year-old but had shown himself a three-year-old of the highest class by his two facile Goodwood victories, and he started a 7–4 chance at Doncaster. Second favourite, ridden by Steve Cauthen, was the Aga Khan's Baynoun, winner that year of the Queen's Vase at Royal Ascot and the Geoffrey Freer Stakes at Newbury. The field also included another Aga Khan runner in Shernazar, a half-brother to Shergar, as well as two trained by Guy Harwood – Alphabatim, winner of the Guardian Classic Trial and the Highland Spring Derby Trial, and Crazy, winner of the Ebor Handicap. At Talaq had won the Grand Prix de Paris after finishing fourth in the Derby, and French challenger Mont Basile had won four races during the season.

This was the initial running of the world's oldest Classic under commercial sponsorship, and for the first time the winner's prize money topped £100,000. But in truth the field was disappointing: only one runner (At Talaq) had won a Group One event and only four of the others had won any Pattern race. But as an occasion it promised much, for Lester Piggott was idolized by the racing public and expectations were running high that Commanche Run would bring him the record. It was wholly appropriate that to

*Commanche Run beats Baynoun.*

reach this landmark the jockey would have to produce one of his greatest efforts.

Librate, pacemaker for Alphabatim, took the field along at a strong gallop as far as the straight, a good half mile from home, where he fell back and allowed Commanche Run to take up the running. In typical Piggott fashion the pace was steadily increased, until three furlongs out Commanche Run was going for all he was worth, closely pursued by Shernazar and Baynoun, with Alphabatim and Crazy close enough if good enough. Commanche Run responded courageously to pressure from his jockey, and by the final furlong he and Baynoun, running equally gamely, had the race between them. Both were hard ridden but neither flinched, and throughout the final hundred yards Commanche Run kept just ahead of his persistent challenger to prevail by a neck. Alphabatim was third, one and a half lengths behind Baynoun, with Crazy fourth.

It had been a hard-fought victory, and Commanche Run did not race again that season. The following year he developed into one of the best European middle-distance

horses of the 1980s, winning the Brigadier Gerard Stakes, the Benson and Hedges Gold Cup and the Phoenix Champion Stakes before being comprehensively beaten by Pebbles in the Champion Stakes. Baynoun ran only once as a four-year-old (finishing fourth in the John Porter Stakes) before being exported to the USA. Of the subsequent careers of the other runners in the 1984 St Leger, perhaps the most interesting is that of At Talaq, who won the Melbourne Cup in Australia in 1986.

Whether Darrel McHargue would have won on Commanche Run is irrelevant, for this was vintage Lester Piggott – the jockey completely at one with his horse, pushing it just enough to achieve maximum effort but always keeping it balanced, willing and galloping straight for the line. The trials and tribulations which beset Piggott after his riding career was over – imprisonment in October 1987 for tax fraud – do nothing to distract from his achievements in the saddle, and never have his skills been better demonstrated than when he won his twenty-eighth Classic.

**Holsten Pils St Leger Stakes**

Doncaster
1 mile 6 furlongs, 127 yards
15 September 1984

| 1 | Commanche Run | L. Piggott | 7–4 fav. |
| 2 | Baynoun | S. Cauthen | 5–2 |
| 3 | Alphabatim | G. Starkey | 7–1 |

*Also ran:* Crazy (4th), At Talaq, Mont Basile, Shernazar, Librate, Prime Assett, Destroyer, Get The Message

11 ran

Winner owned by I. Allan, trained by L. Cumani

*Distances:* neck, 1½ lengths

# LESTER PIGGOTT AND SIR IVOR

*Washington DC International*
*Laurel Park, 11 November 1968*

*Sir Ivor (left) nips through to lead Czar Alexander (right) and Fort Marcy (blinkers).*

---

**Washington DC International**

---

Laurel Park
1½ miles
11 November 1968

| | | |
|---|---|---|
| 1 Sir Ivor | L. Piggott | 19–10 fav. |
| 2 Czar Alexander | J. Velasquez | 21–10 |
| 3 Fort Marcy | M. Ycaza | 38–10 |

*Also ran:* Carmarthen (4th), La Lagune, Petrone, Azincourt, Takeshiba-O

---

8 ran

---

Winner owned by R. R. Guest, trained by M. V. O'Brien

---

*Distances:* ¾ length, nose

---

❛ *I knew a bit more about Sir Ivor than they did* ❜

Sir Ivor was the first Epsom Derby winner to race in the USA since Papyrus in 1923. He duly won the Washington International, but the race did little for harmony in transatlantic racing relations, for Lester Piggott's handling of the colt provoked a bemused American press into heaping criticism on his apparently indifferent head. The controversy still goes on. Was this one of Piggott's finest hours, riding his horse with such supreme confidence that he was able to win despite encountering traffic problems at a crucial stage of the race? Or was he so inept that Sir Ivor was nearly beaten unnecessarily?

Owned by Raymond Guest and trained in Ireland by Vincent O'Brien, Sir Ivor came to Laurel Park as probably the best European challenger there had yet been for the Washington International. He had won three of his four races as a two-year-old, including the Grand Criterium at Longchamp, and as a three-year-old had taken the Two Thousand Guineas Trial at Ascot before beating Pet-

ingo and Jimmy Reppin in the Two Thousand Guineas itself and then producing a telling burst of speed to win the Derby from Connaught. Defeated in his next four races – the Irish Derby, the Eclipse, the Prix Henry Delamarre and the Arc – he returned to winning ways at the end of the season when cruising home in the Champion Stakes at Newmarket.

Despite those defeats his form was of the highest order, and he was favourite for the International, his odds of 19–10 at the off being slightly shorter than those of the American horse Czar Alexander. Fort Marcy, who had won the race in 1967, was third favourite in a field whose eight runners bore witness to a truly international contest. Apart from the two Americans and Sir Ivor from Ireland, from France came Carmarthen, third in the Arc, La Lagune, winner of the Oaks, and Petrone, facile winner of the Prix Henri Foy; from Argentina, Azincourt II; and from Japan, Takeshiba-O.

After days of heavy rain and snow the

*Owner Raymond Guest with Sir Ivor after the race.*

going on the grass track at Laurel Park was soft, conditions very much against Sir Ivor. Although he had won the Derby, plenty of people were still convinced that he did not truly stay a mile and a half and that Piggott's sensitive handling of him at Epsom, producing him at the very last moment, had masked this lack of stamina. Soft ground would put stamina at a premium over the twelve furlongs, and doubts about Sir Ivor's getting the trip contributed to Piggott's tactics.

Takeshiba-O made the early pace followed by the two American horses Czar Alexander and Fort Marcy, while Piggott was content to keep Sir Ivor well covered up at the back of the field with La Lagune. This order was maintained as the runners came past the stands and started to make their way along the back stretch, and with half a mile to go the field was tightly bunched. Coming round the final turn Takeshiba-O dropped away rapidly and was soon in last place, with Petrone and Azincourt likewise back-pedalling. Sir Ivor came smoothly round the retreating horses to take third place on the rails behind Czar Alexander, with Fort Marcy on the outside. For a moment Fort Marcy grabbed the lead, then Czar Alexander took it back. Carmarthen was a close fourth, and as he made his challenge he completed the box around Sir Ivor. Now they were in the home stretch, and Sir Ivor seemed hopelessly hemmed in as the American horses pushed for the wire. Then, as they came inside the final furlong, Piggott got the break he needed. Carmarthen drifted to the the centre of the course, Fort Marcy ducked in towards the rail, and a gap had appeared. With one brief spurt of acceleration Sir Ivor was through it. Under the whip, he spurted past Czar Alexander shortly before the line and went a length up before Piggott, the race won, dropped his hands. At the wire Sir Ivor had won by three quarters of a length.

This had been Sir Ivor at his brilliant best, striking with one deadly burst of speed. But the American press, used to seeing horses flat out from the start and going at it hammer and tongs, were not in tune to the subtleties of Piggott's unleashing that burst, and the criticism started. Although Joe Nichols in the *New York Times* wrote that 'Lester Pig-

gott rode with the competence that has stamped him as one of the world's great riders, and brought his mount home in time', the *Washington Post* thought that 'there could be fault-finding with Piggott's tactics in tucking in on the rail and not asking his mount for more of the effort he had in reserve'. Gerald Strine in the same newspaper was more forthright: for him Piggott 'nearly got the best horse beaten'. Also in the *Post* was a quote from an anonymous jockey who proclaimed: 'That was the worst ride I've ever seen. He was running up horses' rears all the way round. He shoulda won by fifteen lengths.' And an anonymous journalist: 'If he were an American jockey he'd be crucified.'

Piggott tried to explain. 'If the turf had been hard,' he said, 'we'd have won by a hundred yards,' and then elaborated about Sir Ivor:

*He started gawking at the people in the stands when he came into the stretch. For a second I thought it might be a struggle. But I got after him and he got his mind back on business. We were never really boxed in. But the course was too soft for him. He just wasn't getting hold of it too good. I just had to leave him alone.*

Trainer Vincent O'Brien put it more succinctly: 'Once he got the opening – ping!'

It is just as easy – and as pointless – to criticize the American press for misunderstanding the Piggott style as it is to criticize Piggott for flirting so dangerously with defeat. What really matters is not how the horse won, but that he did win, and that in doing so he ended his racecourse career displaying that sparkling but short-lived turn of foot for which he will long be remembered.

For Lester Piggott himself the differences with the American press were simply answered:

*I didn't think they were qualified to make any judgements. I knew a bit more about Sir Ivor than they did. I also knew the going was very soft. I knew what I had to do.*

*Twenty-one years later at Claiborne Farm in Kentucky, Sir Ivor can still laugh about it all.*

# FOINAVON

Grand National
Liverpool, 8 April 1967

Pat Buckley rushes to help his
stricken mount, Limeking.

**❛ This was an awful
race ❜**

Popham Down was a 66–1 outsider for the 1967 Grand National – a decent price for a horse who three years previously had won the Scottish equivalent at Bogside – but his backers did not enjoy much of a run for their money. Landing over the first fence he crashed into the prostrate form of the faller Meon Valley and was brought down. He struggled to his feet and, free of his human burden, galloped after the surviving runners. A few minutes and twenty-two fences later Popham Down would secure for himself a notorious footnote in racing history . . .

There were forty-four starters in the National that year. The 15–2 favourite was Honey End, ridden by Josh Gifford. Second favourite at 10–1 was Bassnet, with Freddie, a gallant second to Jay Trump in 1965 and second again to Anglo in 1966, third favourite at 100–9. Anglo himself was 100–8 to repeat his victory, and on offer at the same price were Kilburn, The Fossa, and Different Class, owned by Gregory Peck. Among the apparent no-hopers at 100–1 was the blinkered Foinavon, a tall, well-built nine-year-old gelding accompanied to Liverpool by his constant companion, Susie the goat. Foinavon had come a remote fourth in the King George VI Chase at Kempton Park the previous December but few disputed that his starting price in the Grand National was a true reflection of his chance. Foinavon had

not won for two seasons and was considered a plodder and a sketchy jumper – hardly the type for the rigours of the National. Charles Benson in the *Daily Express* on the morning of the race had baldly written: 'Foinavon has no chance. Not the boldest of jumpers, he can safely be ignored, even in a race noted for shocks.'

Foinavon had been trained by Tom Dreaper in Ireland for Arkle's owner Anne, Duchess of Westminster, but while in Dreaper's charge had been notable mainly for his extraordinarily laid-back demeanour: in a chase at Baldoyle he was in the lead when falling at the third fence, throwing Pat Taaffe well clear, but Foinavon did not bother to scramble to his feet, preferring to remain on the ground and pick quietly at the grass beside him. Tom Dreaper could not convince him that racing was a business to be taken seriously, and Foinavon had been sold for 2,000 guineas. He was now trained at Compton in Berkshire by John Kempton, running in the colours of Cyril Watkins. Kempton usually rode the horse himself (and had done so three weeks before the Liverpool race when Foinavon was last in the Cheltenham Gold Cup – at 500–1 – behind Woodland Venture), but his normal riding weight of ten stone ten pounds was way above Foinavon's Grand National mark of ten stone, and so John Buckingham was engaged for his first ride in the great

past the stands for the first time, with most of the runners still surviving, he had few behind him. Approaching Becher's Brook on the second circuit Freddie and Different Class were moving into challenging positions behind the leaders, who were accompanied by two loose horses. Foinavon was plodding along towards the rear, but not that far behind the favourite Honey End, whose jockey Josh Gifford had not been tempted by the furious early pace and who was still running well within himself. The leaders – Castle Falls, Princeful, Kapeno, Rondetto and Rutherfords – swept over Becher's and made for the twenty-third fence, the smallest on the course and, though taken at a left-hand angle, a simple preliminary to the trappy right-angled bend to the left at the Canal Turn. It was now that Popham Down wrote his footnote. After parting from his jockey Macer Gifford at the very first fence he had continued with the rest of the field all the way round, clearing every obstacle and keeping with the herd. He had leapt with ease over the fearsome Becher's Brook on the second circuit, but he was tiring and had no jockey to keep him going. At the twenty-third he decided that enough was enough. Galloping towards the fence on the inside, at the stride before take-off he veered to the right, slamming into Rutherfords, whose jockey Johnny Leech had no chance of staying aboard. Immediately behind, the leading group on the inside crashed into Popham Down and Rutherfords. Limeking went down as if shot, and his rider Pat Buckley desperately tried to get him to his feet as the horse, flanks heaving, lay in a mess of thorn and fir and mud. Other horses slid to the ground. Different Class went down in the melee, and behind him horse upon horse piled into the scrum. Some forced their way through to the landing side of the fence, but without their jockeys. It was chaos. Horses which a moment before were just off the pace crashed into the leaders, tipping off their riders and running up and down the fence, preventing any of the horses following from getting over it. Some skidded to a halt and deposited their jockeys on the landing side. Most simply stopped. Horses careered into the fence and sent gorse flying in all directions. Unseated

TOP *Confusion reigns, but Foinavon (stripes, right) is on his way as Josh Gifford (white sleeves, hooped cap, right) wheels Honey End round for another go.*

ABOVE *With a furlong to run the favourite Honey End is still in hot pursuit of Foinavon, but the shock result cannot now be averted.*

Liverpool race. On National day John Kempton also had a runner at Worcester – Three Dons in a novice hurdle – and opted to take the ride there: having duly won, he settled down in the jockeys' changing room to watch the National on television, safe in the knowledge that his father Jack was at Liverpool to supervise Foinavon's forlorn attempt. Also watching on television, at home, was owner Cyril Watkins. They would not easily forget what they saw.

The race was run at a tremendous pace, and Foinavon was soon feeling the strain. Having been in the front rank at the first fence he dropped back, and as the field came jockeys were scurrying around and fighting madly to reunite themselves with their mounts, but even as they clambered on board there was nowhere to go. The Grand National had been brought to a halt.

John Buckingham on Foinavon, well behind this chaos, was still keeping an eye on Josh Gifford on Honey End, though he was aware that his mount would be likely to prove more one-paced than the favourite. But as Honey End was among those baulked, Buckingham seized the initiative and pulled Foinavon to the outside. He has described the moment which put him and his mount into Grand National legend as they approached the twenty-third fence:

*I was just far enough behind not to get caught up in the thick of it. I had to make an instant decision, so I steered Foinavon to the right – the outside – to get away from the main part of the melee. There was a small gap in the fence that was unaffected by the pile-up and we approached it at a forty-five degree angle. At that stage I had no idea whether anyone else had jumped the fence or not and I was purely concerned about carrying on if I could possibly could. Foinavon had reduced to a canter and he jumped the fence off his hocks like a showjumper. I kicked on away from the fence and realized then that we were in front.*

Foinavon was the first horse over the twenty-third and found himself in a very long lead. He set off for the Canal Turn in glorious isolation while behind him the rest of the field manically tried to salvage some hope from the disaster. Josh Gifford wheeled Honey End round, took him back a few paces and put him at the fence a second time. Terry Biddlecombe on Greek Scholar did likewise, Brian Fletcher remounted Red Alligator, Pat McCarron tried time and again to get Freddie through the sea of flailing legs and eventually did so. Now it was simply a matter of whether the embarrassment of a Foinavon victory could be headed off, but he was thirty lengths in the lead turning away from the Canal Turn and showed no signs of giving up. Gifford on Honey End rode like a man possessed, but as Foinavon sailed over

Valentine's Brook and the next three fences and made towards the stands the pursuit seemed hopeless. And so it proved, for the horse with no chance was not going to accommodate the pundits now: Foinavon jumped the last two and set off up the run-in still twenty lengths to the good. Gifford never gave up and seemed to be making an appreciable dent on the gap, but at the winning post Foinavon was still fifteen lengths in front. Red Alligator, who was to win the National under more orthodox circumstances the following year, was third and Greek Scholar fourth. In all, eighteen of the forty-four starters completed the course.

Mindful that the shenanigans at the twenty-third would do little to enhance the image of the Grand National, then at a low ebb, the Stewards of the meeting were moved to issue a statement:

*As a result of a leading loose horse running across the fence after Becher's on the second circuit (the 23rd), there was a pile-up and Foinavon was the only horse to jump the fence first time. The remainder of the finishers were either remounted or put to the fence a second time.*

Whether such a statement did much to repair the damage is questionable, but the jockeys and trainers did not mince their words. An exasperated Josh Gifford claimed – with much justification – that 'I should have won by a furlong. 'For Ryan Price, trainer of the favourite, 'Honey End was robbed'; for Peter Cazalet, 'This was an awful race.'

The complete freak result? Foinavon's effort deserves a better entry in the roll of Grand National honour than that of the luckiest winner in the history of the race. For while his victory certainly overturned the basic tenets of any horse race – he won because he was so far behind at the crucial moment – still he gained that victory by adapting to the circumstances which had suddenly presented themselves, by his jockey's quick and skilful manoeuvring by his jockey, by jumping accurately and by keeping up his gallop to the end.

Foinavon should not have won the 1967 Grand National. But he did.

**Grand National**

Liverpool
4 miles 856 yards
8 April 1967

| | | | |
|---|---|---|---|
| 1 Foinavon | J. Buckingham | 100–1 |
| 2 Honey End | J. Gifford | 15–2 fav. |
| 3 Red Alligator | B. Fletcher | 30–1 |

*Also ran:* Greek Scholar (4th), Packed Home, Solbina, Aussie, Scottish Final, What A Myth, Kapeno, Quintin Bay, Bob-A-Job, Steel Bridge, Castle Falls, Ross Sea, Rutherfords, Freddie, Game Purston, Rondetto, Different Class, Anglo, Kilburn, Limeking, Bassnet, Officious Horn, Forecastle, Meon Valley, Lucky Domino, The Fossa, Norther, Dorimont, Kirtle-Lad, Popham Down, April Rose, Vulcano, Dunwiddy, Penvulgo, Leedsy, Princeful, Ronald's Boy, Border Fury, Harry Black, Aerial III, Tower Road, Barberyn

44 ran

Winner owned by C. P. T. Watkins, trained by J. Kempton

*Distances:* 15 lengths, 3 lengths

# ACKNOWLEDGEMENTS

Without the accommodating support of Michael and Louise Wigley this book could not have been written when it was.

I am also grateful to Robert Cooper for advice; to Dr Alice Hills at the National Horseracing Museum for help and for constant coffee; to the staff of the Newmarket Public Library for regularly surrendering the key to the library's invaluable Racing Collection; to Andrea Stern for winkling out the pictures; and to Gillian Bromley.

A book such as this is constructed from the work of many others. Among those whose accounts of great races I have most heavily drawn upon are Bill Curling, John Hislop, Tony Morris, Roger Mortimer, John Oaksey, Jonathan Powell and Michael Tanner.

S.M.

The publishers would like to thank the following for providing photographs:

Arlington International Racecourse Ltd 86, 87 left, 97, 98, 102

Associated Press 32, 33, 34, 88, 122 top, 128, 139, 140 bottom

P. Bertrand & Son, Chantilly 94, 131, 132 right

British Movietone News 113 (all)

Gerry Cranham 9, 11, 12 top and bottom, 15, 27, 35, 36, 37, 41, 43, 58, 63, 81, 84, 85, 103, 108, 109, 118, 120 bottom, 122, 123, 132 left, 137, 138

John Crofts Photography 56, 78, 121

*Daily Express* 142 top

Jerry Frutkoff 92

*The Herald & Weekly Times*, Melbourne 74, 91

Hulton Picture Company 89, 117, 130

*Illustrated London News* 19 top and centre, 24, 64, 71, 82 top and bottom, 112 bottom, 126, 127

Japan Racing Association 51

Trevor Jones 2, 30, 31, 66, 111

Keeneland-Cook, Kentucky 38, 39

Kinetic Corporation 47

Sean Magee 70, 140 top

Peter Mooney 72, 73, 77

New York Racing Association/Photo Horst Schafer 17, 60, 61

Popperfoto 20, 21, 22, 110, 116, 129, 141, 142 bottom

Racecourse Technical Services 57

W. W. Rouch & Co. 65

George Selwyn 29, 44, 45, 48, 49, 54, 55 top and bottom, 80, 87 right, 119

Split Second 67, 104, 105, 106 top and bottom, 120 top

Sport & General 23, 53, 99, 101, 114

Sporting Pictures (UK) Ltd 68, 124

Syndication International 59, 134, 135, 136